This book is dedicated to my first spiritual directors:
my mother and father.
My gratitude to them for transmitting the gift of Faith and Love
is constant.
And this gratitude is extended to those women and men
who have been my formal spiritual companions and teachers,
and to the many other companions and friends I have met
"along the way."

Contents

Foreword

My heart burned within me as I read this book. To read Eileen O'Hea's *In Wisdom's Kitchen: The Process of Spiritual Direction* is not only to learn about spiritual direction but to actually begin to receive it. Although writing primarily for spiritual directors, Eileen portrays spiritual yearnings, inner struggles, and contemplative joy with such force that the book becomes an invitation to seek the Living One, fully, consciously, with one's whole heart, mind, and strength.

Eileen is bilingual. She writes one story in two languages, the language of prose narrative and the language of poetry. The two modes of speech converge as one multifaceted story of human longing to know God. In both prose and poetry Eileen records the struggles, pitfalls, and benefits of spiritual direction, illuminating the process for directors and directees alike.

In the prose narrative account, Eileen describes various personality types among those who come for spiritual direction. She points to typical snares each type may meet and resistances they may present to the director, and she offers various strategies for leading people to new consciousness. Presented with both male and female characters, these typical cases are like snapshots that depict the enormous variety and vitality of human attraction to the divine and of human stumblings in the spiritual quest. These prose depictions arise from Eileen's own inner process, and from years accompanying her friends toward the Unnameable One.

Eileen's model of spiritual direction is one of mutuality and accompaniment. To describe the relationship of director and directee, Eileen chooses language of friendship rather than director and directee, which imply a hierarchical relationship of domination and subordination. By contrast, "friendship" implies a mutuality of respect and openness between two people. To walk with the friend seeking direction does not mean that the spiritual director can ignore professional boundaries in the work of direction. Instead, the relationship of friends indicates that both director and directee accompany each other in the search for the Holy One. Both must remain open to the Spirit in their interactions, and both must be willing to change, to be surprised, and to discover new life as it emerges in the spiritual process. Friendship between the director and directee implies that the director, though more experienced and theologically informed, is equally engaged in the search for God as the one who comes seeking direction.

Eileen's chapters discuss major themes that emerge in the process of spiritual direction. Forgiveness in Eileen's hands, for example, becomes a movement toward healing that often follows truth-telling. It is not a violent act of the will imposed by religious commitment or the "shoulds" of conscience. Rather, forgiveness is the gentle sign of healing that emerges from painful acknowledgment of past hurt. Forgiveness may lead to the "deepest level of compassion (that) can only be extended by someone already centered in the reality of forgiveness and love" (p. 49).

In *Wisdom's Kitchen*, Eileen brings the contemplative tradition of the five spiritual senses back into the center of spiritual direction. With the analogy of the physical senses, she shows how language of the spiritual senses provides a vocabulary for speaking of internal awareness, openness, and spiritual liveliness in daily life. Using classical tradition, Eileen makes it possible to name inner experience so often left unacknowledged because language for it is beyond reach. Without words, inner life can remain unnamed, unrecognized, and outside of consciousness. Ultimately, Eileen pushes us beyond language to the wordless knowing of divine Mystery, but her words lay out a path, illuminating, beautifying, and guiding.

Eileen's poetic language lifts this most helpful book from the level of spiritual manual to a profound invitation to search for the One "beyond all form." Most chapters contain Eileen's own poetry that startles, even takes the breath away, in the sudden recognitions it evokes. She writes of dullness, of delusions, of unrequited longings. She tells of broken hopes and secret tenderness. She speaks of waiting and of the birthing of joyful fullness.

Eileen's poetry courses through the book, even in the prose material. From Old Testament wisdom texts Eileen draws her most important metaphor for God as Wisdom. Using biblical resources, combined with language of mystics like Julian of Norwich, and of contemporary theologians like Elizabeth Johnson, she brings current theological conversation into spiritual searching. She calls on Jesus as Sophia-God incarnate. She understands life as a kitchen in which Wisdom prepares a feast for us. She claims Wisdom as the "Knitter and Unknotter." Eileen's poetic language breaks boundaries between theological categories and leads readers toward union with the Holy One. This is possible because, for Eileen, all language about God points beyond itself to the unity of all things in divine Mystery.

At the heart of Eileen's book is her own experience of healing, freedom, and unfathomable divinity. Her book soothes, challenges, and invites. At the same time, it does not exclude the pain of suffering, death, and loss but finds through them the compassion of the divine Mother. Eileen urges us to enter into the murky depths of our own violence, hatred, and despair. She calls us to die to our egos and to rise with Christ.

The book closes with an original and engaging model of a dialogue with Wisdom that encourages readers to pursue conversation with her directly. It also includes a chart of typical movements in the spiritual journey. The benefit of such a chart is that it shows readers that rhythms and seasons of their own relationship with Holy Wisdom may not be signs of their own failure or lack of commitment but may represent common patterns in the spiritual life.

It is true that "Wisdom, the fashioner of all things," has taught Eileen. In this book she teaches us to seek her in all the doubts, fears, and beauty of our lives to say "Come O Wisdom Come."

Kathleen M. O'Connor
Professor of Old Testament
Columbia Theological Seminary
Decatur, Georgia

Introduction

In Wisdom's Kitchen is a book about the spiritual direction process. Sacred scripture invites us to look for Wisdom nearby: "You will find her sitting at your gate." This book is about meeting Wisdom as she works in the kitchen of our souls. Kitchens are gathering places, where people tell stories and exchange love and friendship in food preparation, shared meals, and simply being with each other. More frequently than not kitchens are places of fond memories, where hearts open and share both love and pain.

The kitchen is a good metaphor for the spiritual direction process. In this kitchen Wisdom is very active—sometimes more overtly than at other times, but always present and attentive, always ready to serve. Wisdom never imposes her presence; nor does she intrude. Wisdom invites into her kitchen those who are seeking truth, those looking for purpose and meaning in their lives, those trying to make sense of life, those who are spiritually poor and hungry, those whose souls are thirsting for God (Chapter 1, "Wisdom's Invitation").

In the spiritual direction process both the director and the directee come into Wisdom's kitchen. Both connect with what is deepest and truest of themselves because of her. It is Wisdom's presence that weaves the bond of spiritual friendship that connects the person listening or directing and the person (the directee) who has come to Wisdom's kitchen to be nourished. Both will change through this encounter and it is Wisdom's doing (Chapter 2, "Wisdom's Presence: The Spiritual Journey Past and Present").

In Wisdom's Kitchen is a book is about such encounters. Wisdom's invitation always comes first. In Chapter 1 we study Wisdom's call. People hear and respond to it differently. One response is the process of spiritual direction. This book explores the dynamics of that process by allowing the reader to find him or herself in Wisdom's kitchen listening to different personality types as they unfold their stories. Here, the reader will discover ways different individuals seek spiritual direction, and their styles of searching for and acknowledging the presence of divine love in their own lives. Here, the

1

reader will also be able to note how Wisdom operates through the director and what effect the encounter has on him or her (Chapter 3, "At Wisdom's Table: Different Styles, Different Spiritualities").

To be in Wisdom's company is to discover that we, like the psalmist, want to cry out: "I treasured her more than gold" (Wisdom 7: 10). When we journey with Wisdom, we travel through layers of the persona and our own psychological histories until we meet the self free of the impediments that keep us from knowing our own wholeness, loveableness, and goodness. Wisdom leads us into the experience of knowing ourselves held in divine love. Companionship with Wisdom leads us into the experience of contemplative prayer. This pathway of prayer aligns our life and energies with divine life and energies; it takes us beyond thoughts and images *about* God and opens us to the experience of oneness *with and in* divine love. As we sit at Wisdom's table, we explore the contemplative prayer of Christian meditation or "sitting prayer." This chapter invites the reader to share in the experiences and struggles of those seeking spiritual direction and practicing this prayer (Chapter 4 "Companionship with Wisdom: Christian Meditation or 'Sitting Prayer' ").

Forgiving others and forgiving ourselves is a major theme in life and, therefore, a major component of the spiritual-direction process. Chapter 5, "Wisdom: Midwife, Mother, Knitter, and Unknotter" identifies the roots of unforgiveness and some of Wisdom's teaching about liberating the stony heart.

"Wisdom's Ways: The Interior Senses" (Chapter 6) identifies those senses which, flooded by divine light, enable us to experience life at its most profound level. This chapter discusses the awakening of these senses and what happens to individuals when they are no longer available to them.

The experience of *knowing* is a form of knowledge that goes beyond the rational mind and is foundational to all aspects of the spiritual journey. "At Home in Wisdom: Knowing" (Chapter 7) reflects on this experience.

Wisdom's activity in the kitchen of our soul brings with it a variety of spiritual experiences that can affect us psychologically, emotionally, and physically. We delight in many of them; we can also know discomfort and pain as Wisdom draws us through the many transitions that are part of the deepening of our spiritual lives. "Wisdom's Friendship: The Dance of Intimacy" (Chapter 8) helps the reader identify some of Wisdom's activity as we continue on the spiritual journey.

Since Wisdom is the giver of gifts, the "Addendum: A Dialogue with Wisdom" offers a helpful method for aligning our energies and finding peace when we have become uncentered due to some circumstance of life.

About Wisdom

Do not look for her
"waiting at your gate"
as sacred scripture tells you.
Rather, you will find her
in the kitchen of
your soul.
And, when sacred scripture gives
you her qualities,
leading you to believe
that what she does is gentle,
 kind,
radiant,
don't take it literally.
This pure emanation of light
stings, burns, disseminates.
She has a dark side—
although it is
carefully cloaked in femininIty.

I have been deluded.
Learned people have
 presented her to me
as the most eloquent of teachers.
I once believed her lessons
emerged
only in dancing light
and bubbling joy.
I now know there is something
very dull, very deflating "in"
her presence.

I shall rewrite Her story for you—
the true story.
Wisdom is a wine maker;
she presses upon the plucky
grapes.
Wisdom is a kitchen chef;
she takes a ball of dough and
presses it flat.
Presses out its moisture and
its life.

Wisdom is a meat tenderizer;
she breaks the sinews of the ego,
then shapes it to her own liking.
She, my friends, is not quite as
benevolent as we were led to
believe.
And so, when you hear:
 . . . "for companionship with her
has no bitterness,"
know it is not true.

Wisdom levels,
presses down,
makes disappear,
both emotion
and illusion.
She unbalances you;
puts your life askew.
To know her
is to know
you will never experience
disappointment or
disillusionment to the same degree
again,
or
perhaps any other feeling
of deprivation or lack.
And it is Wisdom's fault!
(And yours and mine for letting
her in the kitchens of our souls!)

". . . Since Wisdom, the fashioner
of all things has taught me,"
I'll make public some of her
secrets.
Wisdom abides
beneath our joy,
beneath our sorrow,
beneath all transient experiences—
good and the bad.
In this way she robs us of the

comfort of pure emotion.
Because of her, collapsing into
our disappointment, sadness,
loss of hope, or pain, is hardly
possible.
We are deprived of reveling in
our self-pity.
Deprived of the discordant comfort
we find in personal hurt
—which either activates our
righteousness or qualifies us for
the misplaced attention
our egos crave.

Wisdom flatens
She deflates the ego.
I know, for
today I sit with Her.
It is a very dull place.
I am neither sad nor glad.
Wisdom claimed me today,
disallowing by her presence,
the antics of an ego that
could easily revel in self-absorp-
tion and self-pity.
I am feeling gypped!

I am feeling the absence of
ego-feeling.
I am feeling a little,
 a very little, wise.

Be on your guard my friends,
"For she reaches mightily from one
end of the earth to the other,
and she orders all things well ."
(Wis. 8. 1)

O Wisdom!
Come!
Do your thing
in the kitchen of our universe.
Press out our collective egoism.
Teach us how to order all
things well
—for all women and men
—for our earth
—for all that is.
Come, O Wisdom,
Come!
We need you now.
Come!
Come!

1

Wisdom's Invitation

There are many paths into Wisdom's kitchen. The call of Wisdom addresses the mind and the heart. It is always the same call: Come! Come in! The response to this call always leads to truth and interiority, to the acknowledgment that divine love is the ground of being. Wisdom's call can be experienced as an urge to discover meaning, the desire not to live one's life superficially, or the impulse to express with one's life that divine love is the source and central reality of life. Wisdom's draw is like that of a great magnetic field that keeps moving us more deeply into the discovery of divine Mystery, into the discovery of our true identity.

There are many paths. People encounter Wisdom through reading, through the arts, through various forms of prayer and religious practice, through love and friendship. Her ways are many and cannot be limited. Spiritual direction is one path into Wisdom's kitchen.

What can be known about the encounter with Wisdom and the depth to which she leads us is that we will know the reality of this encounter by its fruits. As is true of all religious experience, the one who encounters Wisdom will know deeper faith, invigorated hope, and greater love. Such deepening and enlivening are always the litmus test of authentic religious experience, but are not to be confused with perfection and faultless behavior in a person.

Many of us who are living into the twenty-first century have found the practice of monthly spiritual direction to be a way of responding to Wisdom's call to "come in" and to "go deeper yet." For others, spiritual direction is still a conundrum. When one inserts the topic of spiritual direction into conversations, it is not unusual for a blank stare to come over the faces of some of those gathered. "I haven't the slightest idea what it is," one person says. Another adds, "I know people undertake direction and talk about their spiritual lives, but it is not something I ever see myself doing. My spiritual life is between God and me." A third member comments, "I can't imagine what people have to say about their spiritual life; if God is Mystery, what's to say?"

Spiritual direction is always about a relationship. It is about an individual sensing that his or her life has meaning and purpose beyond that of ego consciousness; that is, intuiting a call to something deeper, something *more*. Most people, but not all, name this *more* as having its source and origin in divine life in some form. Those not connected to any faith tradition often recognize a life force and a drive toward fundamental goodness, toward being and creating goodness in our world. They experience this as a drive or moral imperative inside of them to make their life congruent with all that is good and true. These individuals seek spiritual direction because they are committed to fundamental values and principles of life and are seeking help in being true to them and to their own processes of growth as interdependent and good human beings.

The experience of the risen Jesus, the Christ, whom John's gospel identifies with Wisdom or Sophia, causes his followers to orient their lives and being to this relationship and the spreading of the Good News. For all Christian believers, the experience of divine life, as revealed through Jesus-Sophia, is the fundamental life principle, the ground of being from which all life emanates, from which all life takes meaning and purpose.

> Christian faith is grounded on the experience that God who is Spirit at work in the tragic and beautiful world to vivify and renew all creatures through the gracious power of her indwelling, liberating love, is present again through the very particular history of one human being, Jesus of Nazareth.[1]

The experience of Jesus-Sophia created a fundamental shift inside of women and men who then wanted their lives to express this experience. We have instances of people in our own time reorganizing the way they live because of some dramatic or traumatic happening that shocked and opened them to a deeper reality, an experience which propelled them to enter consciously into the process of transformation. For example, near-death experiences have caused some individuals to leave the corporate world and then to live more simply and close to the earth. The experience of prison and solitary confinement has caused political leaders and others to reform their lives and values.

In New Testament times, the encounter with Jesus was so powerful and wonderful that people gathered together to express the reality they knew both as community and individuals. They articulated creeds to name what they believed. They created hymns and rituals to express their relationship and response to this experience. They set out guidelines for behavior to help

---

1. Elizabeth A. Johnson, *She Who Is: The Mystery of God in Feminist Theological Discourse* (New York: Crossroad, 1992), 150.

keep them focused on what they wanted their life orientation to be, to help keep them in communion with the experience of Christ. These creeds, codes, and rituals gave Christians ways to stay in touch with the reality they knew was worth their lives, an experience in which their life's meaning and purpose found congruence, hope, and fulfillment. Their relationship with Christ addressed, fed, answered their hunger and desire for the more they had always felt within them. In a word, they found their happiness, experienced as a fundamental oneness of their being in and with the divine Being. This experience was so encompassing, so wonderful, and so life-giving that these people wanted to respond by giving themselves completely, as lover does to lover.

Creeds, rituals, and codes have been passed on through the ages with the intent of helping the Christian community express its collective experience of Jesus Christ's living presence in and among them. However, if forms and formulas have become entities in themselves and have lost touch with the experience for which they were created, then they no longer nourish and vivify the community.

> The community of disciples is charged with keeping alive throughout the ages the good news let loose in the struggling world through the history and destiny of Jesus of Nazareth. An excellent way of doing so is provided by the wisdom tradition, which since the first century has allowed all the power of the figure of Sophia to focus and filter the significance and identity of the Messiah. Jesus is Sophia incarnate, the Wisdom of God: "but she was sent in one way that she might be with human beings; and she has been sent in another way that she herself might be a human being."[2]

Communities that realize Jesus-Sophia's presence long to express this experience. The community is composed of individuals, each of whom possess a particular and personal relationship with the person of Christ. A longing to know Christ and be known in relationship with Christ deepens and intensifies in each person who is awake to this reality. And because this relationship with Christ is primary in their lives, they then try to orient their lives in such a way that the relationship grows and deepens.

A personal prayer life is intrinsic to this relationship. Prayer is both a response to divine love by one discovering one is loved and an experience of intentionality; that is, a deliberate act that reflects the value and priority of this relationship in one's life. Different styles and forms of prayer will reflect the differences in people as they respond to divine love. One prayer form might be helpful at one phase of the journey but not at another, or

---

2. Ibid., 156–57.

forms that were once important to an individual's prayer life might be used
again but with a wholly different understanding. For example, it is not
uncommon for people who prayed the rosary in their youth to return to it
in the mature years.

People enter into a process of spiritual direction because their relationship with divine life is central. For them the spiritual director is a person
who will help them reflect on their lives, help them discover the ongoing
dynamics of this relationship of love, help them discern when their lives are
congruent with their deepest beliefs and values and when they are not.

Good spiritual directors are people who are gifted in recognizing what
is truly of the Spirit and what is not. They are people who are educated to
recognize the dynamics that are part of the spiritual journey. Because they
are sensitive and reflective about their own life, they are able to bring a
depth of understanding, compassion, and care into the spiritual-direction
process. The spiritual-direction process also involves a unique relationship
between the one who is listening and the one who is sharing. Sharing one's
spiritual journey with another means allowing the other into the most intimate part of one's life. Although the director's role is primarily one of
listening to individuals and then helping them discern how and where they
are experiencing the presence of Wisdom, directors also share some of their
own story when doing so facilitates the work of Wisdom.

Over time a friendship develops in spiritual direction that is unique. It
is a friendship between two individuals who meet in or around the Center
of Reality. And although an observer might perceive this relationship as
one of mentor and mentoree, one not fully mutual in the ordinary sense,
nevertheless an experience of genuine concern and love for each other usually
develops. Such friendship does not depend on the usual forms of exchange
for realizing friendship. Their meeting at the Center of Reality, whether as
director or directee, opens each to a communion that goes beyond form, a
communion in being, in love.

Roles, hierarchies, contrasts, and comparisons have no meaning here.
However, the same boundaries that are incorporated into other professional
relationships must be incorporated within each session. This makes good
sense and provides each with the necessary boundaries that allow the process
to work best. The one asking to be heard and helped receives the complete
attention of the other. Directors detach as fully as possible from their own
personal agenda and through this detachment center themselves at a place
where they are available to the direction and impulses of Holy Wisdom.
Freed from their own agenda, they deepen their capacity for listening.

All good spiritual directors know that they are there to facilitate Wisdom's activity in the person before them. In our Western culture the relationship of guru and disciple, terms in the Hindu tradition that denote a

disciple's complete turning over of his or her life to an acknowledged sage or holy person, is *never* part of the spiritual direction process. The guru/ disciple relationship is one of dependence and submission. The director's role, by contrast, is to facilitate, to listen, to give feedback, to share knowledge. In fact, we use the term *director* about a process rather than a role. In the process of spiritual direction the director's role is best described and thought about as that of companion. These companions, or sisters, or brothers, know that it is Wisdom who is our teacher, our friend, our provider, our guru. As companions on a spiritual journey, they listen to our stories, help us identify what is going on in our process, challenge us when necessary about the illusions or delusions they see operating in our lives. These mentors, hopefully, never see themselves in positions of power or authority but as mediators and friends. People seeking direction, therefore, choose individuals whom they sense have a commitment to their own process, people who demonstrate in their lives and being a commitment to divine love and a faithfulness to their life's journey. They are individuals who manifest some of Wisdom's gifts and yet evidence a realness that can only be born from dealing with the struggles and pains of their own lives.

People seek spiritual direction because the presence and feedback from one at home in Wisdom's kitchen enlivens and nourishes what they value most: intimacy with divine love. There are many paths to the same mountain top. Getting spiritual direction is one helpful path for some individuals. For others, Wisdom will meet them in different ways.

Consolation

I did not know
—had no idea—
that in loving you
I would discover
you are loving me
yesterday, today,
tomorrow, now;
and, quite dearly.
Your touch so tender,
your glance consuming,
but never overwhelming—
just there—
if I dare
look up
and meet your gaze of love.

How pathetic my striving,
how foolish my fear
of disappointing you.
You whose name is Love.
You are all that is,
and your love—
sweet, gentle,
an abyss of light
cushioning my soul.

2

Wisdom's Presence:

The Spiritual Journey Past and Present

The process of spiritual direction is about meeting Wisdom, she who sits at the gate of our soul, for the seeker will "find her sitting at the gate" (Wisdom 6: 14). Encountering Wisdom, getting to know her intimately, learning to live in her presence, and being instructed by her is both an ancient and a new image of divine life's abiding presence in human history. Solomon, in the book of Wisdom, instructs us in how to make contact with Wisdom: "Therefore I prayed and understanding was given me; I called on God, and the spirit of Wisdom came to me" (Wisdom 7: 7).

Wisdom, as the feminine of God,[1] can be a welcome metaphor for the experience of divine activity in the hearts of women and men in our modern world. Although our theology and experience teach us that eternal Mystery is beyond form, we as human persons have to use analogies from our experience to express and make sense of the energies of our minds and the responses of our hearts. The images or comparisons used throughout classical theology and up until our present day represent the cultures and values of the historical period in which they developed. God as Father is one such image that has been deeply implanted in our theological and emotional understanding of divine life. Frequently, this representation of divine life bears with it the understanding of fatherhood known in that culture and society, one that may accentuate male privilege and dominance. When we

1. Kathleen M. O'Connor, *The Wisdom Literature* (Wilmington, Del.: Michael Glazier, 1988), 192. "Finally, to recognize that the God whose love and mercy Jesus came to reveal is both Father and Sophia-God, enables us to glimpse less idolatrously, the transcendent and liberating mystery of God."

Ibid., 188. "In the Sermon on the Mount, Matthew identifies Jesus as the true Torah just as Sophia is Torah incarnate in Sirach 24. Moreover, for Matthew the disciples of Jesus are commissioned as envoys of Wisdom incarnate to continue his work."

Ibid., 136. "The all encompassing theme of Sirach's Book is Wisdom or, as she is called in Greek, Sophia."

identify these activities of privilege or dominance with eternal Mystery, they misrepresent it and corrupt the purity of a once wholesome insight. Since divine life is beyond form, any metaphor fails to capture and express it completely. However, every image or analogy is a window into divine Mystery that can express and convey some truth to us. So, yes, God is *like* a loving father, or God is *like* a loving mother. But of its nature, divine love cannot be encased in one or a multitude of images or analogies. Every comparison will tell us something, but it can never hope to tell us everything.

> Holy Wisdom is the mother of the universe, the unoriginate, living source of all that exists. This unimaginable livingness generates the life of all creatures, being herself, in the beginning and continuously, the power of being within being.[2]

Spiritual direction is about being attentive to or awake to the presence of Wisdom in our personal lives and in the world in which we live. We find theological foundations for this endeavor in each and all of the following truths: God *is* with us; we are made *in* God's image and likeness and therefore participate in the very life and activity of God; the same Spirit that was in Jesus-Sophia[3] leading him through his life, death, and resurrection is in us and leading us through our life, death and resurrection; the reign of divine love is dependent on the conversion of the human heart. Without such a conversion, greed, violence, hatred, and egotism can so overwhelm individuals, and thereby the collective experience of the whole, that we delay divine love's reign.

To the extent that we recognize, love, and cherish the activity of Divine Love in us and in our world, to that extent will we know:

1. that each of us is beloved of God;
2. that we are in communion with all beings and with our universe;
3. that we are now the healing, redeeming and liberating presence of Jesus-Sophia in our world, that we are indeed *the body* of Christ;
4. that love of God and love of neighbor are inseparable truths;
5. that our life's task is to become the person God created us to be; that is, to get beyond the ploys, delusions, compulsions, and programs of our egos;
6. that the mission of Jesus-Sophia is set free through us and therefore we are in the process of cocreating our universe in every moment of every day.

2. Johnson, *She Who Is*, 151.
3. Ibid., 150–169.

Wisdom makes known the reality of her presence to us in sometimes subtle, sometimes obvious ways. *Consolation* is the word usually identified with the realization of her presence. Consolation is the experience of knowing the presence of divine life and energy intertwined with our life and energy in either the difficult or wonderful experiences of our lives. It is the experience of knowing love and therefore realizing a sense of peace or joy deep within ourselves, an experience to which our emotions frequently respond.

Desolation is the word used to describe a place devoid of any perceived experience of divine love. Its emotional tone can be compared to being in a lit room and then gradually or all at once finding oneself in utter darkness. Times of desolation are difficult to bear, especially when one is accustomed to some experience of feeling connected to divine love spiritually, emotionally, or in both ways. Consolation and desolation are part of the spiritual journey and therefore each will be the subject matter of the spiritual-direction process at different times.

Several scriptural images offer us metaphors that depict the dynamics of the spiritual-direction process. The Israelites' Exodus experience is one. Yahweh frees the Israelites from slavery and invites them to a new land, to freedom. As they make the transition from their place of unfreedom to a place of true freedom, they wander in the desert, an in-between place that brings with it all sorts of doubt, discomfort, and discontent. The desire to return to the past, to go back to Egypt, begins to overshadow their initial desire to be free. As they become consumed with their own need for survival, they forget that Yahweh is with them. They forget in the same way and for the same reasons as each of us on the spiritual journey. Life becomes too hard or we get so absorbed in survival and our own needs that our attention does not take us beyond our ego selves. Or we assume wrongly that when the presence of God is not palpable to us or part of our emotional experiences, that it does not exist, that it is not reliable, or that it is not worth our efforts. The spiritual-direction process is about remembering and being awake to divine love's presence in all aspects of our lives—in good times and in bad. The presence of the Divine fills all of life, constantly drawing us from the bondage of our egos to new life and freedom in every experience. The activity and presence of Wisdom draw us beyond what seem like death-dealing experiences—places of no hope, places of too much pain and hardship, places where we could easily give up and despair—to new life that will bring us freedom. Like the Israelites we must remember that Yahweh is with us, will not abandon us, is in fact, despite the obvious appearances of things, providing what we need spiritually. We must learn to keep faith during the difficult and wonderful experiences of life. The spiritual-direction process helps us remember this truth.

ISRAELITES' STORY

FROM:	DESERT	TO:
Egypt and	————————————————	Promised Land
bondage	TRANSITION	*FREEDOM*

MY STORY

FROM:	LIFE EVENTS	TO:
compulsions of	————————————————	New Life
the ego	TRANSITION	*FREEDOM*
(bondage)		

The presence of Wisdom, of Sophia-God, to us and in us has, like all relationships, some identifiable moments. These moments are unique to our personal experiences in this relationship, but are also familiar in the archetypal pool of human experiences found in sacred scriptures and other writings that portray the human search and struggle. These moments make up a lifetime. They are the content of the spiritual-direction process. In the scripture Job represents the archetypal struggling believer.

Job, in the Book of Job, takes *umbrage* with God, wrestles with God, keeps reminding God that he, Job, is being faithful but is struggling to believe because he cannot comprehend how God can act so uncaringly, so dispassionately. Job represents an individual in the experience of desolation. Job's struggle resonates with each of us questioning how suffering can be part of our lives. In Job's suffering we find the question he and we ask God: why is it that bad things happen to good people? Why is it when I try so hard my relationships fail? Why is it that nations suffer? Why is it that in my time of need you seem so unavailable, so unpresent to me, to our world?

Although the book of Job never answers directly the question of suffering, Job gives witness to the reality of God's presence and God's availability in his life and therefore to us in the midst of our suffering. Job can be a model for the spiritual-direction process, because Job in his struggle encounters God in the present. The spiritual-direction process is about realizing our union and companionship with Jesus-Sophia in all of life's circumstances as they occur. Those who make a habit of reflecting on their lives begin to realize that the experience of divine life and energy is present to them even in those experiences of life that are cruel or dreadful. They see this in retrospect. It is this reflective activity that builds a personal faith history. What we find in Job's witness is someone attending to the experience of Wisdom as it is occurring.

Within the spiritual-direction process we, like Job, find a place to vent our anguish and disappointments about life and about God. We, too, in the process remember the reality of Wisdom's presence even in the midst of our suffering. "Job," writes Kathleen O'Connor, "depicts the death and resurrection of the people, the revivifying of collapsed relationships, and the overthrow of doctrines and ideologies which prevent full human life in communion with God."[4]

Job depicts the necessary deaths that are continually going on in all aspects of our lives, and therefore in our spiritual lives as well. We must continually detach or die to our preconceived ideas about holy Mystery and about life. We must, like Job, remain in faith and hope—a process that can withstand our tantrums, our outbursts to God, and our railings against injustice. Spiritual direction is about such a process. It provides us with the opportunity of being heard and understood in our pain, and helps in distinguishing the voices of hope from those of despair.

In the process of spiritual direction we remember our own faith histories as well as those of our ancestors, such as Thérèse of Liseux, John of the Cross, Clare of Assisi, Ignatius of Loyola, and so many others. A study of their lives and suffering reminds us that each time one of them entered into a death experience in faith, as when Ignatius of Loyola experienced a conversion of his life while enduring a terrible sickness, new life resulted. These many ancestors of ours help us realize that for us as well new life comes when we detach from our ego world, from its perceptions, judgments, obsessions, addictions, and whatever locks us into a mind state or way of being in this world that is death-dealing. Our own faith histories attest to this. Through our own remembrance or the director's recalling of some faith experience from our past, we invigorate our hope in the present circumstance as we recall that new life followed the loss and darkness that surrounded facing into death in some previous form. For instance, we recall how difficult it was to admit to some wrongdoing and then ask for forgiveness, and we remember the experience of peace and freedom that followed.

In the New Testament we find the dynamics of the spiritual journey and the presence of Wisdom laid out before us in many places. The story of Martha and Mary, for example, identifies the experience of consolation. The death of their brother Lazarus leaves both women in a place of deep grief and sadness. When Jesus-Sophia calls Lazarus forth from the tomb, their joy seems immeasurable. And with this experience, their faith, which was deep before this occasion, knows new depths. An increase in faith, in hope, in love always characterizes true religious experience.

Jesus said to her [Martha], "Did I not tell you that if you believed, you would see the glory of God?" (John 11: 40)

While in Wisdom's kitchen, we quickly discover that her activity takes unique forms. Her ways and tools for leading and teaching us are limitless. In the Hebrew scriptures, for instance, Wisdom very directly and dramatically intervenes with Habakkuk, whom she lifts bodily and by the hair of his head from one geographic place to another. In more subtle but similar ways, Wisdom's activity can have the same effect on us; we are, as it were, lifted out from our ordinary experience and into another realm of experience that words can't adequately describe or contain, in which profound joy or peace or love seems to fill every fiber of our being. Mystical experiences in which persons know themselves (and this usually after the fact) completely absorbed in divine life or contemplative prayer that draws them into a place of "unknowing," are examples of this.[5] We cannot induce these experiences or make them happen. They are pure gift. We cannot cling to religious experiences for their own sakes, as a source of pride or self-aggrandizement. We can only enjoy them as one enjoys the gift of flowers. We do not devour the flowers, clutch them, or pull them apart to see how they are made. Rather, we allow their beauty and fragrance to nurture our souls and remind us of the good and the beautiful. Mystical experiences, religious experiences, contemplative experiences are gifts given to deepen faith, hope, and love, to nurture us on the journey.

In the process of spiritual direction we share our stories, and we remember those times when we were awake to the encounter with Wisdom that is continually going on in our lives. In the dynamic of this remembrance, as in our prayer lives, we continually move into deeper levels of awareness, deeper levels of consciousness. Our personal lives—our friendships, encounters with others, and all other forms of relationship, namely, with businesses, nature, the universe—are subject matter for spiritual direction. How we encounter life in all its forms is the content of each spiritual-direction session.

5. "There is no longer 'any object' but the drawing of the whole person, with the very ground of his [her] being, into love, beyond any defined circumscribable object, into the infinity of God as God himself. [herself]" Karl Rahner, "The Logic of Concrete Individual Knowledge in Ignatius Loyola," pp. 132 ff., cited from *The Best of the Review* (Review for Religious: St. Louis, Mo. 1983), p. 7, n. 3.

There are times in our lives when we meet the resurrected Christ in ourselves or in others. We, like the women and men disciples in the gospels, experience the joy that comes with such encounters. At other times we, like Thomas, encounter the wounded Christ in ourselves or in others. We find Christ wearing the wounds that we have denied or blocked from our consciousness. We encounter these wounds when we begin to dislike or even hate someone because of the hurt they have inflicted upon us. Often their goodness disappears from our sight, and simultaneously our hearts get hardened as our egos become obsessed with their behaviors. Our own lack of freedom then becomes apparent to us and to the director. We identify this experience by saying that we feel uncentered, lost, no longer at one with ourselves or with divine love. Our experience of injustice or of another's unfair treatment is real and must be dealt with. So, too, must the fact that our personal freedom has diminished and our hearts have become hardened.

Often, if not always, we find within these events the hurts or blocks that have their roots in our early personal histories and which keep us from true liberation. This insight into ourselves extends to other dimensions of life as well. Our biases, our attitudes toward certain cultures, groups, or nations, our prejudices and racist beliefs are scenarios of the same ego dynamic. The unliberated parts of ourselves are frequently projected onto others. The events and relationships that we encounter in life put us in touch with the unliberated parts of ourselves, the blocks that keep us from realizing our true identity. Lifting such blocks out of the hull of darkness, where suppressed or unconscious materials lie, and bringing them to light or consciousness clears away the veils of perceived separation from divine love. Separation is our usual experience when the ego's activity of repression and denial consumes our consciousness. Guilt is always a concomitant experience attached to these mechanisms. Meeting, accepting, and even learning to love our wounds, not for themselves but because they become a place for recognizing Christ who meets us in them, will bring us the joy that Thomas encountered when he could finally believe. Once Thomas could see the wounds his doubt vanished.

Thomas's encounter with the risen Christ is a story of coming into the light. Thomas hardened his heart, not out of malice but because the resurrection experience of Jesus didn't fit any experience within his mind of how life is or works. His resistance melted when he saw Jesus's wounds for himself, setting his faith free from doubt, lifting the veils of separation. Thomas was no longer separated from the experience of Christ. Actually Christ was always present to Thomas, but Thomas, like us, was too bound by doubt and fear (ego blocks to awareness) to realize it.

Spiritual direction is always about coming to freedom, the freedom to be our true selves. It is a freedom that comes from taking out of the darkness all that keeps us from the experience of union with Christ, the one who is the incarnate Wisdom of God.[6] It is a union we already share but do not yet experience due to the dynamics and attachments of the ego.

"What was your original face," the Zen teacher asks the student, "the face you had before your parents were born?" The process of spiritual direction helps us discover our original faces. It does so by leading us to our true self. This discovery awakens us to the reality of our union in and with divine love.

6. "Jesus is Sophia incarnate, the Wisdom of God . . ." *She Who Is*, 157.

Spiritual Direction

a word
again
puts me
  back together
takes a spirit
  broken
draws it
from death
to life

long ago
a Word
spoken
a body broken
arose
visited
places
  of darkness
  despair
  death
setting loose
Spirit

today
a word
again
descends
into
the hell
of self-rejection
setting loose
spirit
freeing it
from life's
black holes

3

At Wisdom's Table
Different Styles, Different Spiritualities

How we experience our world, our universe, our faith, and ourselves is evolving. The expansion of consciousness inherent in this process makes us aware of our place in the cosmos. We are in transition in so many ways that it is difficult to articulate what is going on in us and around us. Confusion, doubt, chaos, and experience of loss are elements of the transitions that those seeking and giving spiritual direction feel. The term *spiritual direction* itself reflects people's ongoing search for a center, for purpose.

Many who have been involved in the process of direction tried to change its name, substituting such terms as *spiritual companionship, spiritual friendship, soul sharing* between two or a group, group spiritual sharing, *faith sharing, companions on the way, mentoring partnerships, spiritual partnering, walking with another*. All of these terms attempt to find a name that presents the process as essentially mutual, one that fosters our western and democratic values of equality among peoples and our desire to promote relationships that reflect mutuality, respect, and communion. Relationships associated with power, dominance, and hierarchy are antithetical to the content and context of the spiritual-direction process, a process that helps us become awake to union with divine love and therefore to our interconnection of being with all that is. Somehow, changing the name *spiritual direction* did not work, perhaps because most people do not experience the process as hierarchical in any way and did experience it as mutual. However, many things about the spiritual-direction relationship are going through their own evolutionary process.

The spiritual-direction process helps us become aware of our God images and awaken to the truth of the reality of divine love's presence in our evolving world and in unfolding ourselves.

How we think about and relate with holy Mystery differs among individuals and groups. Images of God, those formed concepts that identify

God for us and that are often a carryover from childhood learning, very much influence our relationship with the Divine. For example, if we have learned that God is a judge, or one who punishes us, we will fear God and recoil from the personal discovery necessary to our spiritual journey. If we have learned that God is like a loving father and mother, we will enter into a relationship of discovery more easily, trying to discern for ourselves who God is, if God is, and if God is, then what this means in our lives.

Beyond Image

When the astronauts stepped out in space, some say the modern age ended and the transition to global consciousness began. This transition is very much part of the spiritual-direction process itself and the evolution of consciousness that process engages. Our postmodern age is witnessing a new consciousness that propels individuals to take their proper place in the universe, a consciousness that replaces self-absorption and narcissism with self-transcendence, a consciousness that realizes that our personal journey of faith is necessarily both personal and collective and cannot be one without the other. This new consciousness links my personal identity with the world in which I live and the fate of the entire cosmos. The spirituality of the earth, the spirituality of justice, and renewed interest in astrology connect personal identity to the earth, to all peoples, to the universe. Such awareness gives rise to different spiritualities, different methods of prayer, and different social activities and ministries.

In the spiritual-direction process, the director is aware that new ways of approaching and interpreting Wisdom's ways are manifesting themselves in individual and cultural consciousness. The following scenarios represent different personality types, different experiences of the spiritual journey, and different theologies that can be part of the spiritual-direction process. Before the proclaiming of the gospel in the Greek rite, the celebrant sings three times: "Wisdom. Be attentive." Perhaps, as the director listens to the different stories of the friend before her, his or her theologies, practice, and search, she should also hear, "Wisdom! Be Attentive!"

This chapter invites the reader to listen in and to be attentive to thirteen types of personal stories that unfold at Wisdom's table. Each is a dialog between persons seeking spiritual direction and a companion. These encounters include basic approaches the director can take in such scenarios.

The Scenarios: Wisdom! Be Attentive!

Alices and Adams

The Alice or Adam types come for direction to be accountable for what is happening in their lives in the daily specifics of their personal and prayer lives. Alice keeps a journal and refers to her entries as she talks to her spiritual guide. Adam has a few things he wants to cover during this time, and therefore comes with a list. He usually knows what things he wants to spend time on and what things he wants the opportunity to hear himself say out loud. Both Alice and Adam know that spiritual direction is about connecting life and prayer, and therefore take time to say how they have experienced God's presence in their prayer and comment on whether prayer has been hard or difficult. Both are astute enough to realize their prayer lives ebb and flow with their personal lives.

A: "I've felt very antsy, distracted, at prayer."
Director: "What do you do with that feeling? Do you talk it over with God/Jesus-Sophia?"
A: " I tried journaling; that got me no place."
D: "How did you feel about that?"
A: "I felt flat, indifferent."

The scenario continues in a dialog between the director and directee, looking at the experiences of the directee. The director appreciates the As' faithfulness to their own processes and tries to move with them as they explore their life of faith. Frequently, as the session continues the director will elicit from the directees where they sensed they were being challenged or led in their personal life and their responses to the world around them.

Usually by the end of the session the directees have renewed their commitment to hang in there in faith and love and feel motivated to continue the journey. The director also feels that the mutual exchange of faith nourishes her or his own faith life.

Beatrices and Beethovens

For Beatrice and Beethoven, God is the dance of life, and they are dancing! They are very busy people, very involved in committees, social life relationships, and doing good. They do not take too much quiet time for themselves, either in prayer time or in their daily life. Unless they are having difficulty in a relationship or feel their job is in jeopardy, they are feeling quite content with their lives. They often come to spiritual direction feeling as if the visit is interrupting something more important that is going on in their lives. Once there, however, they are glad for the opportunity to report on their lives, almost using the time as a living journal experience.

D: "How have you experienced the presence of divine life and love in your life?"

B: "In all the things I've just told you."

D: "Do you sense the movement of divine life or energy in any particular way?"

B: "I just feel God is in it all."

D: "Do you have the sense then that your life is in the right place?"

B: "I'm liking it."

D: "Is there any way I can be helpful to you?"

B: "I find this helpful. It is good for me to take some time to reflect on my life with someone."

The director in a session like this must discern the movement of Wisdom in herself as well as in the Beatrices and Beethovens. What of his or her spiritual understanding is the director trying to impose on these friends? What is resistance and denial in the Beatrices and Beethovens? What is just a pure lack of depth in the Beatrices and Beethovens? Perhaps the Bs are not ready for direction, do not need direction, or need to see someone else. Or is the director simply called to more patience and a better sense of timing with the Bs?

The Beatrices and Beethovens usually leave the session feeling good, another task of life accomplished, another good thing completed. For most directors this is a difficult scenario because no depth of experience has been exchanged. The directors can experience self-doubt, or impatience, and wonder, "what's it all about?" If directors are not careful, like the Bs they can move on quickly to the next person or next task without identifying their own experience and thereby dull their own inner process.

Cassandras and Carls

These friends do not believe in formal prayer and feel quite all right about that fact. They give time to prayer in many ways each day. Sometimes their prayer takes place in the car as they drive going to work; some days they keep a journal; some days they go for long walks and commune with nature; some days they listen to beautiful music. They do, however, place a high value on having quiet times and reflection times; both are integral to their lives. They articulate that they continually sense God's love and presence in their lives in good times and in bad. They are contemplative by disposition and desire, and they have developed an interiority that allows them to seek and find God in all. This interiority, the ability to go deep within themselves and become one with their own center, has come from the value and time they have given to their interior process.

When the Cassandras and Carls come for direction, the director feels he or she is pulling taffy with a friend. Together they explore how the revelation of God is happening in the Cs' lives. The Cassandras and Carls usually bring some question about themselves, or some insight into God's revealing activity in them or in our world that they have recently come to, or they easily articulate some place in their personal or prayer life where they feel stuck.

C: "I found myself overeating last week, then I found myself spiraling down spiritually and emotionally with thoughts of self-hatred."

D: "Were you able to intervene on that process?"

C: "Finally, I brought it to prayer."

D: "What happened then?"

C: "Once I named and acknowledged it I could move on."

D: "Where was God/Spirit-Sophia in all this?"

C: "Missing in action on the feeling level, but I *knew* that not to be a reality from deep within. That's one of the advantages of age . . . some wisdom!"

The Cs usually leave direction feeling helped and more aware of God in all the facets of their life. The taffy-pull usually causes the director to go deep within herself to meet the Cs and can, because of this, push her to articulate some wisdom or truth within her that she did not know as clearly before this encounter. In these encounters directors experience mutuality in ministry very palpably, which makes the session rich and somewhat easier for the director.

Desdemonas and Descartes

God who? The Ds no longer can talk about God. God to them is Ultimate Mystery. There is nothing to say! They have been on the spiritual journey for a long time and have been faithful to that growing experience. Many have had their spiritual life rooted in a faithfulness to the celebration of the Eucharist, formal prayer, and meditation on the Gospels. They have absorbed the principles and values explicated in gospels and the life of Jesus into their own lives, but they no longer relate to Jesus in the same ways. Jesus is no longer pivotal to their prayer.

The Ds who are feminist no longer go to parish liturgies because they do not find them inclusive, inspiring, or the only way to celebrate the revelation of divine Mystery in the cosmos. These Ds, in spiritual direction, speak of "missing," "loss," and "sadness" about what had originally formed them in terms of formal religion and religious practice. Many keep trying, going back to what was in an effort not to lose what seems so foundational to their being. They return from these experiences disappointed and with their sadness deepened. The forms which once fed them no longer do. They seem somehow pushed back or no longer personally engaged with the Divine. "It" is somehow within and without everything for them, but not in a way they understand, can articulate, or can feel a connection to in a concrete and personal way. That is what is lost. That is what some are grieving.

Some feminists find comfort in discovering the feminine faces of divine Mystery, and their search for the feminine in Mystery motivates and connects them to divine life and energy. Some realize this intellectually; others form an emotional bonding as well.

Grief, loss, and the joy of discovery are main themes in the spiritual-direction sessions, as is the director's questioning about the individual's faithfulness to his or her own inner process. Many of these friends find some form of contemplative prayer, a prayer that carries them beyond form, integral to being faithful to their life's journey.

Since they can no longer relate to most of the forms and structures which once carried them, their spiritual-direction sessions become a place where they experience that their spiritual journey, its pain, search for truth, joy, and discomfort are valued and appreciated. Here friends attend to and acknowledge the transition they are going through. The director helps them look at their transition and its doubts, fears, and assumptions in the context of other shifts happening in our world.

The director during these sessions must value the authentic search going on in the directees and support them in their search. It is not a place for facile solutions to questions about divine life. The director's theological understanding or experience can be part of a dialog that explores some of the questioning involved, but never with the intent of imposing an opinion or point of view. More often than not, the director will encounter in these sessions some of his or her own questions. How these questions become part of our faith lives is an important element of the direction process. Answering the questions is not. The director must always remember (a constant source for humility) that divine life is mystery and therefore can never be fully known, and that different windows into this mystery open to us as we travel our spiritual path.

Evas and Ernests

Evas and Ernests are those friends who have come to spiritual direction faithfully for years, have been faithful to their prayer lives, and have taken their personal process seriously. They have had personal counseling or group work and frequent workshops on areas where they recognize they need growth. They do all this to clear the path so that they can realize, or not block, the experience of divine love. The great overriding sadness of their lives is that they never have had an experience of God and don't know why. They feel cheated, asked too much of, left out. Sometimes these individuals complain of never experiencing love in any form or from anyone. They do not consider the friends that they have intimates. Sometimes these individuals finally do find an experience of intimacy and love, yet cannot identify this with the experience of divine love except in a general way. Often, too, after long and careful study and intervention on primitive family patterns, they seem to grow stronger personally but still sense some deep lack about the experience of divine love in their lives.

Sometimes the Es, because they are so faithful to their spiritual process, will eventually come to the point of letting go of needing an experience of God and deliberately choose to live in faith. Most times, however, even though they resign themselves to this, the director who sees them over the years finds that they still feel cheated or deprived by God.

After exploring every block to some realization of God's love, asking how God's love might be experienced, what that individual thinks this experience is supposed to be, or whether it is of the emotions or intellect or an interior knowing, after doing all of this, and storming the heavens with prayers besides, what is left for the director to say? Will she say, "I don't know why," and as she does so have a deep sense of her own poverty? Hopefully, she will. And perhaps she will share the following quote from a poem by Rumi, or express something similar because she knows its truth.

> ". . . This longing you express
> IS the return message.
> The grief you cry out from draws you toward union.
> Your pure sadness that wants help
> Is the sacred cup."

The Es leave feeling supported in their struggle, knowing they will continue to wage the war between faith and doubt. The experience of talking to a friend who has known spiritual struggles, who keeps faith, and who supports the search and journey, helps the Es. As they leave, the director, knowing their pain, prays: Sweet and Loving One, touch their heart in a way that they can realize it. They deserve it!

Frannys and Franks

The Fs are the steady-enders in the spiritual life, to use an image that comes from growing up in New York City on a block of more than two hundred other children. Among that many children, one finds one or two individuals who don't think it is a punishment to turn the rope continuously as the game of jump-rope progresses. Usually, one had to turn the rope only by missing a jump and getting caught in. The steady-enders were content to turn the rope and not jump. No one thought of inviting them or challenging them to participate more fully.

The Frannys and Franks in spiritual direction can be those people who are faithful to forms, but are not attentive, or attentive enough to their own experiences and to the nuances of the Spirit. When they find a place of comfort, they settle in, loose touch with a heightened sense of consciousness, and are not fully awake to their own lives and the life of the Spirit working through and in them.

An entry from Frank's journal might look like this:

Friday, May 2, 1996
. . . good day. Had lunch with Pat. Fun. Kept diet. Feels good.
Community meeting concluded well.

Journal entry if Frank wrote from an experience of heightened consciousness and not merely as a log of the events of that day:

. . . good day. Morning prayer rushed/distracted. Setting alarm 5 minutes earlier wd. help.
Lunch with Pat. Fun . . . felt good to connect, missed it when we didn't.
Community meeting . . . sensed George's anger about car. I know I need to speak to him and not let this go, or avoid. Talk to him immediately after Liturgy tomorrow.
Where did I sense God's presence today? (1) aware of George; (2) connecting with Pat; (3) tried to be open and present to M. at ministry conference. Irritated by his small vision of things but treated him respectfully.

Some people can live very good lives or at least lives that are harmless to others. We are called to be fully alive, fully awake. Living in illusions about ourselves or with lack of commitment to our own process will not bring about the reign of God.

Franny has done some hard personal work to discover she is both a lovable and likable person. She has learned to do self-affirmations. However, she has carried this to such an extreme that she no longer looks or sees how her behavior affects others. Franny, for instance, accidentally gives someone the wrong meds during her rounds in the hospital. The way Franny deals with this is to say: "So, you made a mistake! You're still a good person!"

Being responsible for our actions, making restitution and apologies to injured parties, admitting failure and mistakes, and trying to undo the harm we might have consciously or unconsciously caused another are actions good people do. They do not cut themselves off from taking responsibility for their actions.

The role of the director in these cases is to invite and challenge the Frannys and Franks beyond the illusions of a pampered ego.

If the Fs are able to uncover some of the ploys of their egos, it is grace made visible in the here and now. Noting this within the spiritual-direction session is helpful. If, as Franny unfolds her story, she can say: "I don't like admitting I'm wrong; I should be more conscious of covering up things and trying to escape consequences," then Franny begins to unmask her habit of denial. Since each of us knows the truth on some level of our being, the Frannys, upon leaving spiritual direction, might sense more integration because they have confronted an illusion of their egos, as when Fanny articulated the truth that she gave the wrong medicine. However, Franny will not always feel good. The spiritual-direction process furthers a sense of integrity, a sense of being welcomed, accepted, and loved for who we are, as well as a sense of knowing that God is indeed present in my story; however, feeling good on an emotional level may or may not accompany this process.

Georgettes and Gerrys

"Been there, done that!" These people come to spiritual direction looking for something outside of themselves that will create a spiritual high. The spiritual director usually senses this external groping for experience and tries to direct the individual to begin to look inside themselves. The Georgettes and Gerry's are not willing to give any time to deep reflection, journal keeping, prayer practice, or anything that will take them within themselves.

They travel from workshop to workshop, snatch at pieces of truths presented, but refuse the inner journey. This can be for a variety of reasons:

1. They are afraid there is nothing inside of them and choose out of their fear not to look.

2. On some level they intuit the deep emotional scars within and the prospect of looking at them overwhelms them. So they run, keep busy, or stay high to avoid the pain they know could emerge.

3. Some have known the experience of such deep pain, through early childhood emotional, physical, or sexual abuse, that they have vowed, unconsciously, never to go near a place like that again. Others have a similar response if they have known the deep pain of depression or burn-out. These dark and terrible places of pain and death without new life are what they now identify as the journey inward or the spiritual journey. Never again! Never again is their stance. That is why the director must have a sense of timing, must know when there is enough of a relationship of love and trust with these friends to encourage and help them enter into the process of looking at the wounds which block them from the fullness of life. It is love that will enable this process, self-love, the experience of being lovable, the reaffirming of God's unconditional love, and God's promise "I am with you," now, forever. The director might, at the point when the Gs can hear it, direct them to therapy so that they might address their pain and suffering more consistently, their wounds might receive the professional attention they need, and the healing that they desire might begin.

4. Bad habits and a lack of motivation. Sometimes people who have been hurt in life claim victimhood as their way of life. In other words, they opt out of being responsible for their lives or the quality of their lives. Someone else is responsible for who they are becoming, either someone they blame who was part of their past or some spouse or authority figure in the present. Their life is about being dependent, provided for, being a receiver and a taker. In spiritual direction, the Gs expect the director to confirm and affirm their stance in life. She, too, is supposed to join the multitudes who are providing for them.

What are you willing to do or contribute to this process? This is a fundamental question that a director should ask in this type of session.

For the director it takes prayer, a deliberate act of the will, and effort to see the Gs as God sees them. She must not get caught in the manipulative habits of the Gs. It takes grace to stay connected, to love the takers, the demanders, to see the behaviors separate from the person. It takes compassion for the deep psychic wounds that are both hidden and exposed at the same time during a session like this.

Harriettes and Harrolds

"Let's do lunch." Too busy. Missed appointments, changed appointments. No time. Frequently with Hs the spiritual-direction session is about other people's stories: the wife or husband, the parish council, the book they just read and the director must get, the confusion at work, the friend they are caring for. All the things that are part of someone's life can be material for spiritual direction. Chatting can be a part of spiritual direction. It, too, is a holy and wholesome act, an important social skill. However, it should not be the whole of the direction experience.

The Harriettes and Harrys can so load down the director with details or peripheral information that she, like the directee, feels lost and overwhelmed. Spiritual direction is not a place merely to vent about or problem-solve the events of the last parish council or community meeting. However, direction can be about the Hs learning how and where they have sensed the movement of the Spirit in them while attending these meetings. It also may provide the Hs with the opportunity to explore what is happening to them in terms of their own personal and spiritual growth because of this meeting. Some questions the director might use are: "How was this meeting formative in your life, or what keeps it from being formative? Were you off-center or on-center, and what got you off- or what kept you on-center? How did your contribution affect the group and the larger vision and purpose of the group? Did the larger vision become subsumed into themes of turf building or power struggles?" How do the Hs see this, and what part did they play in it?

If the director asks these friends if they want to really go deeper with their experience, the Hs can easily feel hurt. They have sought spiritual direction because subconsciously they long for depth and feel unable to reach it by themselves. Finding paths to help Hs do this can be part of the dialog that occurs in the spiritual-direction session. Journal writing on some of the questions mentioned above is one way. Perhaps drawing or poetry might be another way to move the friend inside of themselves. Asking what gospel text expresses where they feel they are is another suggestion. Some individuals need guidance in learning how to express what they are experiencing within themselves. In these sessions the director is continuing to learn to be patient and loving. She or he must remember that a director is not there to cause anything to happen in the individual; rather the director must remember that she or he is there to *facilitate* Wisdom's work already present and vibrant within this friend.

Ivans and Irenes

The Is are alienated from a religious tradition they had followed committedly. The Is now find the revelation of divine life and energy in the cosmos. Their spirituality can not be separated from the world they live in. They connect all life forms—sun, moon, stars, forest, plants, trees, animals, animate and inanimate matter—intimately with themselves. They experience this interconnectedness of being as a dynamic of love and mutuality. These Is carry within themselves an urgency and sense of mission, a call, to bring about right relationships. Their life's purpose has become grounded in the reality of these connections of mutuality, which causes them to call us and themselves continuously to see differently, to be different, to be responsible for and to our earth and all its creatures. They recognize that a shift in consciousness, a cosmic spirituality, is necessary not only to saving our planet but also intrinsic to realizing our full humanity. These are the prophets of our time. They are calling us into a whole different way of relating, not only to each other and other nations but also to a communion in consciousness with all life's forms. It is a call to an experience of love and mutuality, to an experience of realized interdependence with divine life as it is reflected in all that is.

As prophets, as people knowing reality from a cosmic and contemplative center, old spiritual forms and structures no longer fit them. They can feel isolated, lonely, missing companionship, unappreciated. Old forms no longer work for them. They find it increasingly difficult to belong, whether it is at a Sunday ritual, a retreat experience, community gathering, or some other event. They have been led into another way of being and seeing. Now, experiences and structures that once supported them, nurtured them, and provided companionship, no longer do—at least not in the same ways.

Frequently, the spiritual-direction process becomes a place where Is can be heard and understood and where they can renew their commitment. The director tries to support the mission and call of the Is, which puts her in the position of another deep and rich taffy pull. It is easy for directors to be intimidated with the Is (and in other cases as well) since the Is are so steeped in information about the cosmos; the director may not be at their level of expertise. But the director must remember that the spiritual-direction process is not about who has what expertise. It is about sharing, an exchange that goes beyond intellectual knowledge.

Neither their prophetic stance nor the activity of the Spirit in Is can continue if the egos of the Is get in the way. Remaining faithful to prayer and staying centered is essential to their well-being. Ego involvement in a cause for its own sake or for the sake of enhancing one's ego is always a danger. A process of discernment is always part of every direction session, especially in the cases of Is. What virtues are present in the individual: humility? detachment? Or have the Is become arrogant, bombastic, judgmental, unloving in their intolerance of others?

The director helps the Is reflect on their commitment, their personal relationships, and the effects of their behavior on others as well as themselves. If they are true prophets, then the director knows that these friends carry a real burden. The director knows they will experience rejection and loneliness, just as Jesus-Sophia did. The director knows that their process together is always about discerning what is truly divinely inspired and should be acted upon, and what is not.

The director will also experience the challenge of the prophetic stance during these sessions. He or she must be open to the experience of Wisdom addressing him or her directly through these conversations with a friend.

Julies and Jacks

Julies and Jacks spend most of their lives trying to please people, and though all of us want to be liked and find it uncomfortable when we are not, the Js find being disliked a deathlike experience and do whatever it takes to be liked and affirmed. The director must be more sensitive, alert, and challenging with the Julies and Jacks, because these friends also quickly discover how to please the director. They become adept at putting before the director those things *they* believe the director wants to hear and hiding aspects of their life around which they are experiencing shame, guilt, or anxiety.

D: "So how are things going with you?"

J: "Really good. I had a chance to get away to a cabin for a week and it gave me an opportunity for some real good prayer and some journaling."

D: "What is the best way for me to facilitate your process today? What would you like to talk about?"

J: "I thought I would read some of my journal entries to you?"

D: "What would you like me to do?"

J: "Well, I thought you would like to know the things I have been thinking about."

D: "Yes, I would. Perhaps you can choose those parts where you sensed you were being moved toward something new or away from something that was not life-giving for you. Can you identify one of each as a beginning?"

J: "Well, I find being in nature a great experience! All the heaviness just seems to fall away. I feel so peace-filled when I'm in nature."

D: "Yes, I can relate to that experience very well. What do you think keeps you from feeling peace-filled when you are at home or in your ministry?"

J: "I don't know."

D: "Well, what do think would keep anyone from peace?"

J: "Guilt, anxiety."

D: "Are either of these true of you?"

J: "I suppose. Actually, I feel guilty most all the time and for a very long time. I know it is because I have been involved in a sexual and genital relationship for three years. I'm always afraid of being found out. He is still married. I always feel I'm such a bad person. A home wrecker! You are the first person I've told. I've always wanted to tell you but just never did."

D: "It has always been my experience that the truth does set us free. I always feel it a particular grace when someone can come to the truth. Has that been your experience?"

J: "Yes, I remember when I was able to talk about my father in therapy. It was such a relief to get those feelings outside of myself and then to have someone to explore them with."

D: "Perhaps you would like to explore what this experience of guilt is like for you."

J: "Yes."

When this kind of information emerges, the director will explore through dialogue questions, such as how Jacks and Julies

1. feel about the relationship and what effect this relationship is having in their lives and in their prayer;
2. see this relationship in terms of their personal life and values;
3. experience the relationship as life-giving or not;
4. are able to be truthful in this relationship;
5. see that the Spirit is at work in this relationship; what are they being drawn toward or away from via the relationship;
6. see this relationship affecting their personal integrity and other aspects of their life;
7. feel after they have revealed this aspect of their life.

During a session like this the director must stay in touch with her own process as well. Since she has been seeing the Jacks and Julies for several years, it is not unlikely that she will feel a bit duped or angry about being misled by a friend for the three years that preceded this conversation. These feelings will need to be processed, but the director's role in this instance is to facilitate the process of Julie and Jack and, therefore, to set aside her own experience for the time being. The director must discern whether her feelings should ever be part of their process together. Wisdom, age, grace, and some professional objectivity allow directors in this and similar situations to keep seeing the friend with love and openness rather than through the lens of their own personal feelings at the time.

It is an important part of the spiritual-direction process that individuals experience their essential core—their goodness, wholeness, and lovableness—seen, upheld, and affirmed no matter what content they bring to the sessions. It is equally important for the director to maintain a sense of integrity and truthfulness. Addressing inappropriate behavior and challenging and confronting death-dealing patterns in a person's life are all part of a relationship of love between and among friends.

Kevins and Kristans

The Kevins and Kristans live very tidy lives physically, mentally, emotionally, and spiritually. They are very perfectionistic and usually repress a great deal of anger. In spiritual direction they often report on their friendships, ministry, or back pain as entities unrelated to their spiritual life. The role of the director is to help the Ks interweave the strands of their lives. Spiritual direction for the Ks helps them loosen the control and compartments in which they live their lives, softens them, makes their lives and hearts more porous.

The Ks are usually quite hard on themselves and have a tendency to use the spiritual-direction process to report on how they have failed or not measured up in their lives. With these friends the director needs to be a gentle and loving presence, not so much challenging their behavior as encouraging them to appreciate and value their efforts toward what is good, what is true.

Playing back to the Ks their own effort and desires can be helpful to them.

> D.: I do hear you saying that you have found prayer difficult and rather dry. I also hear you saying that you have been very faithful to your prayer each day.
>
> D: On Thursday, when you felt so distracted in prayer, or when your response to your friend was quick and sharp, how was God seeing you?

The director might suggest that the directee spend some time in prayer doing the following: "see God seeing you with complete love." The director, in an effort to change some of the negative patterning, might suggest that Ks practice an examination of consciousness each day by noting each evening three places where they experienced God's love for them, or practice doing three loving things toward themselves each day, such as taking time to enjoy some music, enjoying the company of a friend, or taking a leisurely walk.

Lauras and Larrys

The Lauras' and Larrys' lives have been filled with rich spiritual experiences. They have confidence on their path whether they are in spiritual darkness or great light. Their spiritual histories reveal that they have kicked and screamed at times of darkness, that they have known the dread of divine absence, and that they have also known the divine light infiltrating their heart and their being.

Their prayer and life indicate to the director that integration has happened and is happening. Because of their rich spiritual histories, they no longer grasp at or demand spiritual experiences, and find being open to the dailiness of life a very rich experience.

Laura and Larry frequently talk about their personal relationships and how they see them reflecting the dynamics and revelations of their own spiritual process. Laura, for example, presents to the spiritual director her experience of saying no to a friend. She did this out of her own need for time and space.

> *Laura:* I know I can't say yes indiscriminately, but I wonder if I am becoming selfish. How can I be sure what is of God and what isn't, especially when it is about me?

Larry had a similar concern. He also said no to using his gifts of facilitation with a group. He has suffered from being overbusy in life and literally burnt out several years ago. Now he, too, is finding it difficult to know when his choices are too self-protective, too selfish.

Both Larry and Laura feel selfish saying no. Their quandary during the spiritual-direction process is to discern if this feeling is the result of some family and cultural patterning or a spiritual insight. The Ls have studied the patterns in themselves and their families of origin; for example, they know that saying no to an adult who was making a request of them was not seen in their families as acceptable behavior. Laura and Larry are astute enough to be in touch, at least intellectually, with this patterning, yet emotionally they frequently revisit this place of insecurity and self-doubt. They easily sense the disapproval of those to whom they said no and who may have interpreted their no or boundary as unreasonable and lacking in real care for others. To withstand this judgment, the Ls take a stand inside of themselves, consciously or unconsciously, which makes them feel tough and invulnerable.

In the case of the Ls the director knows that he or she is dealing with people well schooled in the dynamics of the spirit and the psyche. The director knows the *dis-ease* these individuals are feeling is very real and is related not only to this particular decision but also to its deeper roots.

The task of the director in this situation is to *explore*—not to answer yes or no to the dilemma before the Ls or too quickly console or challenge the person struggling with this form of self-doubt. Some of the questions the director might raise are:

- When you make a choice for yourself and it displeases others, do you usually find that in order to help yourself stay with your decision, you toughen up yourself and your heart?
- Do you think there could be a carry over of this emotional experience (a toughened heart) into your personal prayer?
- Do you remember a time when you said no and still felt vulnerable to the other and open to prayer?
- What is different or the same in this case?

The director might, after exploration, point out to the Ls that the yes or no to the questions raised are secondary to allowing their instincts and the movement of Wisdom to become available to them. Frequently we are psychologically, emotionally, and spiritually programmed to have our nos produce guilt and doubt. Only by risking behavioral changes and then processing them over time will we learn which decisions are the result of Wisdom's promptings and which are selfish. The director might also note that our wills and divine love's will might be the same thing, but our processes for knowing this needs time and patience. The interior sense of knowing—a knowing different from intellectual knowledge or emotional feelings—becomes available to us as our journey deepens. Dealing with our doubts and fears is one way in which this window to the soul and its interior knowledge and light are made available to us.

Mikes and Marys

Mikes and Marys plod. They plod through the good times and the bad. Their highs are not that high nor are their lows that low. Ms do not express too much discontent about their spiritual and emotional lives. The director while listening to these friends looks for clues in their stories that suggest invitations to play, creativity, and friendships that might be happening in their lives and could invite them to cross the line of predictability.

Encouraging the Ms to explore some workshop on prayer and dance, or art and prayer, or yoga and prayer, so that the Ms keep broadening their horizons and allow the many dimensions of divine mystery to be revealed in them, might be appropriate. This will depend on the content they offer during the sessions and the relationship of mutual trust that has been established.

The director realizes that leveling off at a place of comfort is never part of the spiritual journey. The director also knows that divine Mystery is always drawing us into fuller realization of divine and human life. The director must, therefore, be alert and awake to the nuances hidden beneath the very ordinary experiences of Mary and Mike. It is easy, especially after a long day, for the director to be lulled with people like Mary and Mike into a place where many spiritual riches are indeed present, but miss the invitation of Wisdom to go deeper yet.

Water Lilies

They sit,
each day,
all day,
just there;
attuned
to night and day,
opened
to what is.

4

Companionship with Wisdom
Christian Meditation or "Sitting Prayer"

Bird watchers set out early in the morning and position themselves in a bird sanctuary, marsh, or wildlife habitat, where they wait patiently for the first sound or appearance of their friends—the birds. They are so still, so attentive, and so alert as they wait for the first sound or movement that the observer might think they are doing nothing or sleeping rather than sitting fully attentive to possibility.

Those of us who practice a form of contemplative prayer called Christian meditation, or sitting prayer, begin each day with a similar body position and attentiveness. In this prayer we sit in a comfortable, upright position; our spine is straight so that our breathing may be deep and unencumbered, our eyes are gently closed. We repeat a sacred word or mantra for the time of this prayer. This sacred word assists the person praying in his or her efforts to let go of or detach from thoughts, feelings, and experiences that usually lock them into a very limited experience of consciousness. Sitters in the practice of meditation open themselves to reality, to the experience of divine love. This experience of realizing, knowing, and identifying with divine love is already within us. Divine love often remains distant, unexperienced, or unknown because of our conditioning or the hurts and wounds of childhood, as well as society's reinforcement of nonreligious, nonspiritual values and beliefs. Our so-called modern world, says Houston Smith in his interview with Bill Moyers, is the first since the beginning of human life to be a nonreligious society. In this light, the practice of meditation is a countercultural experience. Persons who practice Christian meditation, or sitting prayer, open themselves to and acknowledge divine life as the Source of all that is.

Journeying to a sacred center is an ancient practice known to different religions and cultures; it is one still taking place in our modern world. Moslems travel to Mecca, Hindus to the Ganges, Christians and Jews to

Jerusalem. The labyrinth, a series of concentric circles, like a maze, with one of its pathways leading to the center, is a symbol found on the floor of the great Chartres cathedral in France. When war made pilgrimages to the Holy Land impossible for Christians during the Middle Ages, the symbol of the labyrinth was imprinted on the floor of the cathedral as a substitute for their pilgrimage to the sacred place of Jesus' birth. People walked prayerfully on the large mazelike symbol and acknowledged by this walk that Christ was the center of their life—that their life's purpose was about coming home to the Center of Reality.

Surrendering to the Divine Feminine: the Great Mother

Sitting prayer or Christian meditation can be likened to a pilgrimage to the center represented by the labyrinth or to a sacred river such as the Ganges found in India. All rivers have a source. In sitting prayer, we are like pilgrims immersing ourselves in the living waters of love and surrendering ourselves to their source—the Great Mother,[1] the one who has first surrendered herself to us. In this prayer practice, we disengage from forms and thoughts, desires and emotions, and allow ourselves to be submerged in the draw of divine love.

We do this by detaching (to the extent we are able) from the world of our egos and becoming still and silent externally. We become silent and still internally by repeating a sacred prayer word or mantra that will help us gather our scattered energies and allow them to return to their source— the Great Mother.[2]

Many people who persevere in practicing this prayer for twenty to thirty minutes twice a day find this way of prayer a good fit; namely, it provides them with an experience of prayer that answers their contemplative longing. They experience a sense of well-being and congruence as the result of its daily practice. Coming into the experience of divine life changes people. Like the deep shifts that occur in the plates beneath the surface of our earth, these changes are sometimes imperceptible and do not surface in our consciousness until months or years later. However, this practice of contem-

1. Bede Griffiths, O.S.B., in the film, "A Human Search: The Life of Father Bede Griffiths" (More Than Illusion Films, Sydney, Australia, 1993), tells of his mystical experience and an inner voice which encouraged him to "surrender to the Mother." He states that after doing so he was overcome by waves of love. This, for Bede, was the experience of the divine feminine.

2. "God is both Mother and Father. The Oriental tradition has always recognized this. The biblical name for the spirit (ruah) is feminine and in the later Syriac tradition which preserved the same name the Holy Spirit was spoken of as Mother." Bede Griffiths, *The Universal Christ* (London: Darton, Longman and Todd, 1990), 8.

plative prayer takes us beyond the rational mind and therefore beyond seeing the mind as the only legitimate way of assessing our experience. In sitting prayer the windows of our interior senses open to Wisdom's presence and another type of knowing becomes available to us. This knowing validates our experience and encourages us to persevere in our practice.

Christian meditation (contemplative prayer) not only provides those practicing it with the fruits of prayer and nourishment for their life journeys, it also provides individuals with a way of responding to love. When we awaken to the knowledge that the divine One loves us and that this love is unconditional—that we are loved as we are and for who we are—this experience of knowing we are loved impels us to respond. This is true in our human relationships as well. When we find ourselves in the experience of mutual love, we find in ourselves the desire to give the other something—a gift—to express or to symbolize what we are experiencing toward them. As our spiritual journeys deepen, as we know greater and greater intimacy with divine love, our desire to respond to this love intensifies. Eucharistic celebrations, hymns, psalms, and prayers of love and petition are communal expressions that address our desire but do not fulfill it totally.[3] "Falling in love," being led into the discovery of union with the divine Other, is an intimate and personal experience that yearns to express itself in a response that is also personal.

Each meditation period provides us with a way of making a response of love to love. Each time we practice Christian meditation we, through the process of detaching from our rational minds and our ego self, surrender ourselves totally to the divine Other. Each prayer period becomes a way of saying: You are not only the center of my life; you *are* my life.

In the opera *Samson and Delilah* each lover echoes his and her experience of the other in a beautiful aria: "At the sound of your dear voice, my heart opens." Each meditation period can be thought of as similar to this aria. It is the response of one who loves to love. It is the outpouring of love by one who has realized, on some level, that divine love has first loved them. It is the gift of self given to the Giver of gifts . . . to the One who has given herself completely to us.

To an observer, the daily practice of meditation can seem like a perfunctory and routine task, a daily habit like exercise. It can seem as though it is only a task which makes one feel better about oneself because the mind and body have quieted down and have become less frantic, less controlled

3. Psalm 63: 2–9
   "God my God, you I crave;
   my soul thirsts for you,
   my body aches for you . . ."

by outside stimuli. But what has led the meditator to this practice today and all previous days and years is the *experience* of faith and the *experience* of love. In the lives of the meditators this means they sense, intuit, or realize on some level the presence of divine life at the center of their being. On some level or levels of their being, perhaps through their interior senses, the experience of Christ, or the experience of the Great Mother, seeps, oozes, bubbles, gurgles into the fiber of their being. The experience stokes the fires of hope within each individual for the fulfillment of union with divine love, and each meditation period remembers the meditator to the reality of divine love's presence and to the desire to be discovered in that presence. St. Anselm of Canterbury describes nesting beneath Jesus's wings:

But you, too, good Jesus, are you not also a mother?
Are you not a mother who like a hen gathers her chicks beneath
    her wings?. . . .
And you, my soul, dead in yourself,
run under the wings of Jesus your mother
and lament your grief under his feathers.
Ask that your wounds may be healed
and that, comforted, you may live again.
Christ, my mother, you gather your chickens under your wings;
This dead chicken of yours puts himself under those wings. . . .
Warm your chicken, give life to your dead one, justify your sinner.

—Anselm of Canterbury[4]

Christian Meditation and Spiritual Direction

Question: What does the spiritual director do during the direction process with the person who practices this form of contemplative prayer?

In contemplative or sitting prayer the pray-er comes to the prayer time not looking for experience of any kind but practicing detachment. Through the use of the mantra or sacred word the pray-er detaches from thoughts, feelings, ideas, desires. Teachers instruct the pray-er that during the time of this prayer, even if they have some unusual experience, whether phenomena of the body or of the mind such as an insight or a lucid dream, they should, as soon as they become aware of their mind wandering, continue their prayer by gently returning to their sacred word and continuing to detach from all

4. *The Prayers and Meditations of St. Anselm,* quoted by Johnson, *She Who Is,* 150.

experience. So, in a sense, nothing happens during the prayer time. Nothing is supposed to happen! At least not something that the rational mind determines or registers at the time of prayer.

During the spiritual direction process, directors listen attentively to the friends before them as they relate how they feel about their lives since their last meeting. What friends relate may comprise such things as where they feel they are in a particular relationship, how they have been handling life and ministry, and where they may have noted specific signs of Wisdom moving them toward or away from some event, person, circumstance, or activity. This reflection might include such experiences as saying no to a friend in a relationship in need of some clear boundaries, or yes to taking a stand for peace and justice, a stand which results in making his or her personal life uncomfortable. Exploring the events and circumstances of an individual's life and noting where and how Wisdom is present is always part of the spiritual direction process. Discerning with friends where Wisdom calls them to growth and transformation is integral to this process.

Although the person may use contemplative prayer as his or her structured prayer experience each day and although the pray-er seeks no experience within the prayer time, the director nevertheless invites the friend to talk about this experience. This happens in a variety of ways.

Question: When nothing is supposed to happen during prayer, how does one discuss it?

In the process of spiritual direction the director can explore and dialog with the person who practices Christian meditation questions such as:

How do you see the experience of meditation relating to your daily life?

What are the joys and gifts of the practice of Christian meditation? Are there fruits of this experience emerging in your life?

What are the struggles and disheartening moments that emerge from this prayer experience?

How has meditation influenced your relationships? Your experience of your self? Your professional and work life?

Do you sense any growth or transformation in your own life? Where? How?

What is it that keeps you committed to this practice?

Where are you in relationship to Christ? To sacred scripture?

Who is God for you at this point of your life? How is this experience related to meditation?

How do you begin and end each meditation period?

Are there other forms of prayer that you also employ?

Is the experience of praying with a group helpful to you? Is there a
group you go to or would you like to experience meditating with
a group?

There are a variety of ways of exploring one's experience of Christian
meditation or sitting prayer. The following are a few examples of what such
conversations might sound like.

Example A

Director: Let's talk about your prayer time more specifically. How is
it going for you?

Nancy: The same.

Director: How do you feel about that?

Nancy: All right, I guess. I just do it. I'm usually pretty faithful.

Director: What keeps you so faithful?

Nancy: I feel better about myself when I do it. My day seems to go
better because I'm in a better place.

Director: What place is that?

Nancy: I feel more centered, more in touch with the real me.

Director: Why do you think that is so?

Nancy: I guess my energies seem aligned with divine energy. And
that's what I like and want for my life.

Example B

Director: How is your prayer going?

Terry: What prayer?

Director: Do you want to talk about what is going on there?

Terry: I guess I just gave up. I'm tired of trying and getting nothing
back.

Director: Is that what it has been like for you?

Terry: Pretty much.

Director: Is there a feeling that can match that experience?

Terry: I'm just tired of nothing.

Director: Is this experience particular to your prayer or are you feeling
this way about the rest of your life, too?

Terry: I suppose it is the whole ball of wax. I'm the primary caregiver
for my mother. I see her deteriorating and it is just so hard to
witness. It doesn't seem just or fair that she has to suffer.

Director: (Explores mother's condition, extends compassion for Terry and mother. Director also asks how this is affecting Terry's life in terms of time commitments, health.)

Director: Is faith helpful to you at this time?

Terry: Suffering is such a mystery to me. I don't get it.

Director: Yes, I have similar feelings. I think one of the hardest things in life is to watch someone we love suffer and feel we can do nothing about it. I feel we can handle our own suffering better then seeing the ones we love suffer.

Terry: It has gotten so that I dread going to see my mother, and as soon as I get there I measure how long I'll have to stay.

Director: How do you feel about that when that happens, Terry?

Terry: Guilty, of course.

Director: What do you do with those feelings?

Terry: You know me. I stuff them, pretend they are not there.

Director: What else could you do with them?

Terry: Name them, face them, deal with them.

Director: You might like to journal about them by dialoging with your guilt or fear.

Terry: It is helpful just talking about it. Journaling could help too.

Director: You know Terry, sometimes I think we project onto God some of the experiences of ourselves, or think that if we are not liking who we are or how we are being with our own mother, God must feel that way about us as well. Your theology, I know, is better than that, but our minds can set up these emotional mind sets that situate us in an experience of ourselves that is not true: namely, that we are bad, or lacking, or failing ourselves, our mother, and God. Sometimes, the way we handle our experiences of self-hatred or discontent with ourselves is by creating distance with God, by resisting prayer.

Terry: That's a pretty good sketch of me.

Director: How do you think God sees you at this time?

Terry: My head tells me with complete love but that is not how I feel.

Director: What I would suggest to you then is to take some time to journal. Use whatever technique will help you to explore all your feelings at their deepest level. Then, when you feel you have them all out there, take your journal to your prayer place opened to this dialog. Create a simple ritual, perhaps just placing your open pages before your icon. This way you are acknowledging who you are at this time, you are letting your feelings surface, and you are realizing that these feelings which you don't like or don't want, do not determine who you are at the core of your being, nor do they in any way interfere with the flow of divine energies intermingling with your life. As you can learn to love yourself and be compassionate with yourself, the blocks to the realization of God's utter and complete love for you will disappear.

Example C

Director: How is your prayer time?

Pat: Good. I've gotten to look forward to it.

Director: How is that?

Pat: I feel drawn to it each day. I'm no longer thinking about whether I feel like it or not.

Director: Can you say something about the experience of being drawn?

Pat: Well, when I was reading the scriptures of Holy Week last year, I heard, as if for the first time, Jesus say to Peter, James, and John: "Come pray with me, watch with me." I heard that as an invitation to me. It has somehow seemed to me since then that I accompany Christ, that Christ's prayer continues because I am praying in this world now. Actually, each time I sit down to pray now, it feels like coming home. It is as though the energy that is me returns to its source. It is both a healing and renewing time for me.

Director: How would you describe your response to divine love at this time, Pat?

Pat: I'm just so grateful.

Director: Does this experience get expressed in any way?

Pat: Funny you should ask that. The other day I took a day of prayer. I found myself so overwhelmed with gratitude that I put on a CD and danced my thanks. I've never done that before. I went with my instinct.

Director: It sounds like it served you well.

Example D

Quincy: The first thing I want to talk to you about is my prayer time. I've really been struggling with it.

Director: What's going on?

Quincy: I feel restless and full of distractions. I just can't settle down the way I used to.

Director: That happens to us sometimes.

Quincy: Well, I'm not liking it.

Director: It might be helpful to look at the externals of your prayer time first. Why don't you tell me about your morning prayer time? Tell me everything that happens for you until the end of prayer.

Quincy: I get up at 5:30 A.M., go to the bathroom, and turn on the coffee. After that I open the door of my apartment and pick up the paper, then glance through it quickly as the coffee is finishing. When the coffee finishes, I pour myself a cup and move into my prayer space in the living room. Sometimes I straighten it up a bit because I like to have the space orderly when I pray. After that I sit down on the couch, read the scriptures for the day, and press the timer to begin meditation. I then close my eyes and begin to say the mantra: *Ma ra na tha.* I usually don't get far before I am distracted by the list of things I have to get accomplished that day. And, if that does not take over, then I find myself in la-la land. When the timer goes off, I get up and eat my breakfast. That's about it. Any suggestions? Is there anything you see that could be helpful? At this point I'll try anything.

Director: Well, I could make some suggestions. I think the external circumstances around prayer can influence our interior disposition, and I also believe the reverse is true. Let's focus our attention on the external piece for now. Sometimes, for "morning people" coming to prayer as directly from rising as is possible is very helpful. The fewer distractions the better. The first thing you might try is moving as soon as possible to the place of prayer, not glancing at the paper. The second is having the space ready for prayer. I was wondering if you have a sacred space?

Quincy: I did. I used to have a nice quiet corner near a big window in the sitting room. It was the space I used for prayer. Lately, the cat and her toys have taken over the chair and the space around it. I can rearrange things now that I think about it.

Director: You might want to consider that. The sacred space we create for our meditation times helps situate us in an ambiance for prayer. It can be quite simple and one that suits you. Different people's space for prayer will suit what will please them aesthetically. Initiating the prayer time by lighting a candle is a good ritual for many people. Since most of us live with a limited amount of space in our homes, lighting a candle or burning incense or some other ritual can create the ambiance needed for our prayer.

Quincey: "Yes, I get what you're saying."

Director: Is there anything else going on in your life that you think might be causing your restlessness during prayer?

Example E

Director: How is your prayer time, Rich?

Rich: Not good, not bad!

Director: Do you want to help me understand that?

Rich: Well, some days are better than others. On the good days I put in the full thirty minutes, on the other days I just quit when I find I'm too distracted. It seems dumb to just sit there.

Director: Do you see this as helpful to you?

Rich: Not really. Actually, for the last two weeks or so, now that I think about it, I haven't once finished; I just figure whatever is supposed to be happening isn't happening to me.

Director: What is it you think is supposed to be happening, Rich?

Rich: That I'll strike gold, I guess. Have some experience of God or peace.

Director: This is a very simple way of prayer, Rich. But it is very difficult. During our prayer time we do not look for experiences of any kind. Trying to still the mind that is like a factory always producing thoughts is hard work. Some times are easier than others. But we do it because eventually through practice we will realize a deep peace and a sense of union with Christ.

It is not something we earn by practice, but practice is necessary to clear away the path into this reality that is always available to us, but which we don't experience or don't experience in the ways we think we should. We do experience the fruits of prayer, but we realize these fruits outside of the meditation time itself.[5]

Let me ask you this, Rich. Why do you keep trying?

Rich: Good question. I've asked myself the same thing. I guess it is because I like myself better when I do pray. And despite what I've said, I see this as a way of prayer for me. I guess that is why I've stayed with it.

Director: What I would strongly suggest, Rich, is that you set the timer and stay with the time pattern you have chosen. To give your attention to your restlessness before the period for prayer is

---

5. In Isaiah 32:15–17 we read about the Spirit-Sophia and these fruits:

". . . the wilderness becomes a fruitful field,

and the fruitful field is deemed a forest.

Then justice will dwell in the wilderness, and righteousness abide in the fruitful field.

And the effect of righteousness will be peace,

and the result of righteousness quiet and peace forever.

My people will abide in peaceful habitation, in secure dwellings and in quiet resting places."

over is to accentuate your discomfort. Returning to the mantra at times like this is a death experience, a surrendering in faith. We die to the ego and its distractions and allurements. Whenever we enter into death in faith, no matter what forms of it we are talking about, whether it is the death that comes at the end of life or the dying to the ego that is part of the meditation process, we will find new life.

Rich: What new life do you get with meditation, then?

Director: That is something unique to you, Rich. Something you will have to discover, however, not during your meditation but as you look back on your day. The fruits of Spirit-Sophia are increased faith, more hope, and greater love. Meditation helps us wake up to the activity of divine life at work in ourselves and in our world. Perhaps during the next weeks you can ask yourself each day: Where or when have I experienced greater faith, hope, or love? Is it connected to my contemplative prayer and the stilling of my ego during this time? Let's see what you discover.

Rich: This has been real helpful to me.

Example F (Talks about frustration of prayer)

Director: I hear you saying that staying with meditation has been very difficult for you during the last month. How do you end your prayer, Sandra?

Sandra: I just quit.

Director: Do you feel drawn to another way of prayer?

Sandra: No, not really. It always winds up the same for me. I think I'm just not a good pray-er.

Sandra has the overall feeling about prayer that she has about many other things in her life, namely, that she doesn't do it right. Consequently, she leaves her prayer time with a very subtle but real experience of distaste: distaste for her own efforts, for her own experience, and for prayer itself. Over time there is a very good chance that she will become so discouraged that she will stop praying all together. The director might choose to use some part of this session as a teaching moment in the direction process.

Director: It is important to remember, Sandra, that prayer is not about doing it right. Each prayer period is like sweeping leaves on a path. Some will always blow back. We are not trying to create a perfect path, a path of no leaves. We are trying to say to divine love, "Here I am, as I am, trying to be as open to you as I can be.

Receive my efforts to respond to you, to your love." To become discouraged about your distractions, or restlessness, and then to just leave the encounter with distaste and disappointment in yourself is to discount yourself and divine love's presence to you, whether or not you are experiencing this presence in your emotions or not. If we are out raking leaves on a beautiful fall day, our attention is on the wonder of the season and the beauty that surrounds us. Meditation is essentially about a relationship, a relationship of love, one that is more beautiful than anything we could imagine. Often, when we find ourselves immersed in nature, our hearts impel us to praise and thank the Creator of the universe for such beauty. As we end our meditation the same thing is true. Some will profoundly bow as a gesture that acknowledges this relationship of love; others might say some closing prayer of thanks. And they do this no matter how distracted or empty the meditation time is because they know this time is not to be judged or evaluated through our ego consciousness, which has an investment in comparisons, evaluations, and judgments. Rather, their very last act is to transcend self-preoccupation and spiritual narcissism by acknowledging the relationship of love, a relationship that does not depend on doing it right. To just quit is to allow our ego consciousness to interfere with the relationship, or, to use our metaphor, to become so preoccupied with the leaves on the raked path that we neither value nor experience the wonder and beauty of fall.

Example G

Ted: I'm tired of giving. I want comfort. I want something back.

Director: Are you talking about your home life or your prayer life?

Ted: Both, on some level. But I feel as though I haven't gotten any spiritual perks in a *very* long time.

Director: What is it that you want, Ted?

Ted: I want consolation! (As Ted says this, his eyes fill up with tears. The director knows something is taking place within him. Ted raises the fingers of his right hand indicating to the director that he needs a few minutes.)

Director: (Says quietly) Take as much time as you need, Ted. (She waits without moving, reverencing what she realizes is a profound moment in Ted's life. Several minutes pass. The director waits for Ted to speak first.)

Ted: I just had the strangest experience.

Director: (Notices Ted is visibly quiet, subdued, reverent, in touch with a deeper reality.) Feel free to talk about it or not, Ted. Or, if you need more quiet time or want to leave the session, know that is fine also.

Ted: No, I want to talk about it. I don't know if I can. You see, right after I said I wanted consolation, I had the sense of the divine feminine, right here. It was like having my eyes shut and then realizing a presence of someone close to me even though I didn't hear her approach. I felt the presence. (Hesitates, and is quiet again.)

Director: Sounds like you received a real gift.

Ted: Yes.

(The director waits. She does not try to fill in the quiet spaces that interweave Ted's reflections.)

Ted: I just feel so grateful.

(Quiet)

Ted: I feel so affirmed by God.

(Quiet)

This was so wonderful. I know it will be part of me all my life.

Director: Do you feel consoled?

Ted: That and then some. It seems strange that something like this is happening to me.

Director: What does that mean?

Ted: Like I wanted something, and then I got it.

Director: What exactly did you get?

Ted: An experience of divine love. I feel heard, like my whole being has been responded to by divine love. It's awesome.

Director: I am happy for you, Ted. I'm also grateful you could share it with me. It is a lovely gift.

Ted: That's how I feel.

Director: What is it you would like to do now, Ted?

Ted: I'm not sure. I think I'd like to be quiet for awhile, maybe go for a walk.

Director: Yes, this is a special time, a time to revere your experience. Why don't we close our session now, then?

Ted: Yes, that sounds like a good idea. I need a little time.

This scenario highlights the experience of consolation and the role of the director when the friend before him or her is experiencing this reality. Since words cannot adequately relate the experience of one grasped in the experience of love, conversation does not flow easily in the direction session. The director's role is to be a faithful witness to the experience of the friend and neither to dissect nor explain the experience in an effort to find his or her role during the session. The director listens attentively and supports the friend by being a loving and discerning presence. She or he does not impose her or his thoughts on the friend, and practices the virtue of waiting: that is, of being attentive without intruding on the experience. It is often much harder for directors to be with someone in consolation than desolation because their role is less defined in the former situation.

Ted's religious experience was a more dramatic happening than other religious experiences that occur within the spiritual-direction sessions. However, when someone leaves a session no longer feeling self-hatred because, through unraveling her story with a friend, she once again realizes Mother-Sophia's unconditional love for her, or when one's heart, once hardened or stuck in feelings of hatred against another or himself, is once again open to the experience of love and compassion, these too are religious experiences; these, too, are the result of Wisdom's drawing us into the experience of love.

Wounds

The setting:
a friend
a meal
a guest.
The context:
engaging
friendly
warm.

Then,
the unplanned,
the uninvited
the unexpected.
Some word,
  story,
   look,
opens the wound
covered by time
and drops me
  into its abyss.

5

Wisdom: Midwife, Mother, Knitter, and Unknotter

You created every part of me,
knitting me in my mother's womb.
For such handiwork I praise you.
Awesome this great wonder!

You watch every bone
taking shape in secret,
forming in the hidden depths.

You saw my body grow
according to your design.
You recorded all my days
before they ever began.

                                        Psalm 139[1]

In hymn 139 the psalmist tries to portray how intimately we are connected to divine Mystery and what a tender and loving relationship we have with her. Her activity in the kitchen of our souls is constant. As midwife, she is constantly drawing us through the birth canals integral to the death and resurrection mysteries which are part of daily life. Our willingness to forgive or be forgiven is a major theme in the process of spiritual direction and one where we meet Wisdom as midwife. There are many places on the journey where individuals can get stuck and be in terrible pain because some old or new wound blocks them from a full and vital life. Past wounds can keep us locked in unhealthy mind sets or themes of deprivation that prevent us from moving on and becoming all we are meant to be. Present

1. *Sing Praise: Morning Prayer and Evening Prayer*, compiled by Franciscan Sisters of Perpetual Adoration (La Crosse, Wisconsin, 1992), 563.

wounds have the same effect and are usually rooted in the past and buried in the unconscious. Wisdom's gentle nudges, her firm proddings, her steadfast presence give us the courage to face the dark and to dig ever deeper into the psyche, so that the psychological, spiritual, and emotional patterns that keep us unfree or blocked may be brought into the light and healed. This is one of Wisdom's main tasks. She is a knitter. She knits us back together, back to our original wholeness and lost innocence. She does this when we are ready to face the truths that must be faced. And she does it with great love and patience. She helps us undo our knots, our blocks. She is the mother who holds the hurting child as she assures us that all will be well.

Forgiveness can set loose in an individual some of Wisdom's greatest teachings. The first and most obvious of these is that the truth will always set us free. The second is that although we can practice some form of compassion toward others, only someone centered in the reality of love and forgiveness can extend the deepest level of compassion. The third great teaching that we assimilate from Wisdom takes the longest to understand and is the hardest to accept. It can seem both nonsensical and paradoxical. We forgive people what they have *not* done to us.

During the spiritual-direction sessions in which forgiveness is an ongoing issue in the directee, one of the spiritual director's roles is simply to be a compassionate presence, and thereby to allow the truth to emerge without shame or blame. The director's role is not one of judge, policeperson, or problem-solver. It is Wisdom's work to undo the knots within an individual, and it is the director's role to facilitate this process by listening and supplying some questions that encourage the telling of the truth. If the director, while listening, focuses on a behavior too soon, he or she may short circuit the process or divert it too quickly toward an area that might need attending, but only after the whole story has been shared. Asking too many factual questions would be one example of this. When did this happen? Who was with you? How often did this happen?

As the truth emerges, the first step in the healing process begins, namely, breaking through the taboos that keep us from telling the truth. We ingest taboos from family, church, culture, or society. Taboos lock the gate on secrets we repress or suppress and tether us to our ego consciousness, where we then identify ourselves as bad, unworthy, shameful, hateful. Tremendous fear surrounds our secrets. We fear being found out, cut off, and isolated from those we love. "If they really knew me, knew my past, saw me act in certain ways, then they would know what a phony I am, know how bad I really am." The threat of exposure is a constant and heavy burden. It tortures the psyche with self-recrimination and self-loathing, which frequently perpetuates the vicious cycle of fear, guilt, and shame; feelings which are then alleviated through acting-out behaviors of compulsions and addictions. These, in turn, increase and perpetuate the syndrome and the cycle of sin, fear, guilt, and shame.

When the sun rises on a still lake, the water becomes transparent to certain slants of vision. As the spiritual-direction sessions move along month after month and an individual's prayer life deepens, he or she becomes more interiorly still. The individual then becomes more awake to the repressed and suppressed materials of the past that beg to be acknowledged and brought into the light. This is Wisdom's activity in the kitchens of our souls. Frequently, the spiritual-direction session becomes the first place directees acknowledge their hidden and dark material. Like those standing before a still lake, they begin to *see* the rubble and rocks beneath; that is, they begin to name their truth as they tell their story. By telling and sharing truth, we participate in divine life, no matter what the content. The spiritual director always recognizes this moment of truth-telling as a privileged moment. Directees, often unconsciously, look at the director more closely after revealing some secret, wondering if the director will now see them with the same loathing as they have seen themselves. Good spiritual directors will never indicate any negative reaction, not because they suppress it, but because they genuinely love the individual before them and know his or her goodness. Good spiritual directors also know how to separate behaviors from the essential goodness of the person. Assuring individuals of this fact during a session where a hard truth has been identified is important.

The second step in the healing process takes us beyond seeing and naming our stories; it centers us in the reality of love. We must deal with all the hardened places or blocks in our psyches. Sometimes, depending on how grievous and deep these wounds are, the spiritual director will advise psychotherapy. This process will excavate the hurts from their dark recesses. It is important to see psychotherapy as another room in which Wisdom works. It, too, is a path to the discovery of the deeper self and consequently, like all the other events and circumstances of life, part of the spiritual journey.

A good spiritual director knows that "we are going to do it until we do it." This means we are going to deal with our wounds until they are healed. Some wounds that we thought were healed open up again, given the right circumstances. Examples: The alcoholic who has been in sobriety for fifteen years moves to a new location, stops going to AA meetings, and soon finds himself caught again. Or the person who has dealt effectively with codependent issues and then finds that a new relationship brings to the surface some of the same codependent behaviors. Or the person who feels her anger was healed during three years of intense therapy, during which she identified that she was abused by a parent. At the death of the abusing parent she finds her anger surfaces again and is projected, abusively or subtly, into other relationships.

A spiritual director knows that psychological and emotional wounds need as much or more time to heal as our physical wounds and traumas. Directors know time and patience are always part of the process. They know that when a grace is given it is given completely but that it takes time for the knots rooted in the dark and deep corners in our psyche, those patterns, mindsets, or behaviors, to be unknotted and transformed. The deeper we venture into the depths of ourselves the more clearly we see the rocks or knots that still must be excavated or untied. This dimension of the spiritual life, we are more in touch with our wounds, is not, as many directees are quick to judge, a sign of regression, but of moving deeper into the experience of the true self. Frequently, directees get discouraged when they keep meeting some of the same problems or issues repeatedly. They want to be finished and are impatient with the process and with themselves. When this is the case, it identifies a very human desire for completion but also can identify a compulsion or drive for perfection, which once again alerts us to the fact of the ego's subtle and insidious attachments even to spiritual progress.

True spiritual depth alerts us to the fact that the more closely we identify with our deepest self and experience oneness with divine love, the more we will realize and see where we ourselves are not loving. It is at this point that true humility begins, and it is here that new avenues of knowing divine Mystery open up to us. We begin to know divine life as merciful because of our own need for mercy; we begin to know divine life as compassion because of our need for compassion. Concomitant with these experiences is the realization that divine love is always loving us and that this love is not dependent on what we do or what we fail to do. Over time we begin to realize we are loved for who we are and that our *being* is all that is necessary. It is this experience of love that changes us.

Once we know we are loved to this depth, then our self consciousness and world consciousness begin to change. Making amends for how we have hurt others or being more open to those who have hurt us ensues from this religious experience. Wisdom has awakened us to the fact that love is the beginning and the end of everything. No one in the grasp of divine love will ever hurt another person. It is impossible. Those who project pain onto others or into themselves do so because they are experiencing hurt inside of themselves.

If the second of Wisdom's teachings becomes part of our *knowing,* then the third follows quite easily from it and is neither nonsensical nor paradoxical to us. Once we have discovered that we are in love, that we are indeed loved ultimately by divine life and that nothing changes this reality (the only thing that does change is that we know it at deeper and deeper levels), then we also know that nothing can be taken from us. Why? Because we have found that we have everything. "The everything I longed for is the everything I have found." This truth allows me to deal with life from a very different perspective, one that realizes that nothing can be taken from me. We can still feel the experience of deprivation and diminishment on the level of body, mind, and emotions; for instance, my reputation certainly can be destroyed and I certainly can be subjected to abuse and even torture. This was the case with Etty Hillesum, a young Jewish woman, who died in November 1943 at the concentration camp of Auschwitz. But like her, I will realize that my I, the who that I am, is whole, holy and in divine oneness no matter what other events or tragedies are part of my life story. The entry in her diary for August 18, 1943 reads:

> Sometimes when I stand in some corner of the camp, my feet planted on your earth, my eyes raised towards Your Heaven, tears sometimes run down my face, tears of deep emotion and gratitude. At night, too, when I lie in my bed and rest in You, oh God, tears of gratitude run down my face, and that is my prayer. I have been terribly tired for several days, but that, too, will pass; things come and go in a deeper rhythm and people must be taught to listen to it, it is the most important thing we have to learn in this life. I am not challenging You, oh God, my life is one great dialogue with You. I may never become the great artist I would like to be, but I am already secure in You, God. Sometimes I try my hand at turning out small profundities and uncertain short stories, but I always end up with just one single word: God. And that says everything and there is no need for anything more. And all my creative powers are translated into inner dialogues with You; the beat of my heart has grown deeper, more active and yet more peaceful, and it is as if I were all the time storing up inner riches.[2]

Etty's experience explicates the reality of our oneness with divine love, of finding the everything we long for. Her bliss is not dependent on external circumstances. Etty's interior experience of oneness with divine love does, however, transform how she experiences the horrors of the concentration camp.

Oneness with divine love is oneness with truth, justice, mercy, and compassion, and, therefore, does not lead to passivity or denial in the face of injustice or personal affliction, but does change how we deal with them. If, for example, we are the subjects of violence, abuse, and injustice, our re-

---

2. Etty Hillesum, *An Interrupted Life: The Diaries of Etty Hillesum, 1941–1943* (New York: Washington Square Press, 1985), p. 255.

sponse to these and other world atrocities can not be in kind, although we must respond to them. Our discovery of knowing ourselves at ever deeper levels leads us to the realization that only hurting people—people not in touch with their essential natures, their goodness, wholeness and lovableness—inflict pain on and hurt others. Hurting parents hurt their children. Hurting children hurt other children. It is a learned response by individuals and countries, which comes from a wounded psyche—personal, collective, and cosmic—that tries to rid itself of its sense of deprivation or powerlessness by possessing and dominating others, their lands, their goods, their sense of autonomy.

Every problem, therefore, individual or worldwide, is at root a spiritual problem. The root of all problems is that we don't know who we really are. The knots, the stones block our awareness. We haven't yet awakened to the fact that love holds us and we have everything. This awakening brings with it the experience of realizing our interconnectedness of being with all that is. In it we know we are kin and treat each other with love.

Wisdom's third and greatest teaching is this: we forgive others what they have not done to us. This means that eventually we realize that no one can ever take away our greatest discovery, our most comforting reality, the experience of the truth found within us. No one can take anything away, nor diminish in any way what we have discovered at the essential core of our being, namely, that we have everything. The consequence of this truth is that forgiving others becomes less difficult and less of a block, because beneath almost all acts of trying to forgive others is the belief that they have taken something essential from our person. It can *feel* like this. However, like Etty Hillesum, we must distinguish personal survival and need from the destruction or diminishment of our essential nature.

The process of spiritual direction helps directees disentangle the experience of deprivation and diminishment known to them physically, emotionally, spiritually, or socially from the experience of wholeness and goodness that is their essential nature. This can be a long and difficult process.

The director must be aware that the blocks or knots, many of which are learned patterns of thinking and believing, must be attended to. Otherwise, we remain blocked from the experience of finding ourselves in the arms of love and knowing our own lovableness and goodness. A helpful exercise for the directee who is finding it difficult to forgive someone is to have them talk about or write in their journal on the question: What is it that was taken from you? As the directee explores the many layers of response to this question, the director will hear replies such as: my reputation, my dignity, my possessions, my self-esteem, my self-worth. It is here the director encourages directees to articulate their experiences and their feelings about their losses. The director will recognize that before him or her sits a hurting person who needs to express and explore this experience with someone who is loving and compassionate. Only then can the directee do the work of separating out this pain and its ramifications from the experience of knowing that his or her essential goodness remains intact and that one's essential nature cannot be destroyed or diminished.

This same process is essential in learning how to forgive ourselves and let go of a past that keeps us living a life consumed by self-hatred and self-recrimination for the hurts we have caused. When we discover our essence lost and found in divine love, true compunction ensues. Restitution, taking responsibility for the hurt we have caused others, is the natural response to this discovery. The excavated blocks and the untied knots free us to reestablish relationships and make amends whenever possible.

Contemplative prayer is essential to this awakening because this way of prayer moves us beyond our ego consciousness and situates us in an opened response to the embrace of love. It is here, in the embrace of love, that we realize nothing has been taken from us. It is from this place that we are able to extend the compassion we ourselves have received and are able to forgive ourselves and forgive those who have wronged us. It is from this contemplative space that we are able to forgive others what they have not done to us, because we, like Etty, realize that our *I* lives unscathed and very much in love now and always.

The Wait

This place of darkness
  is eternal night.
A place rich
  yet
vacant,
devoid of light.

Here,
  senses ooze,
evaporate into space.
Nothing is tasted,
nor heard;
Nothing felt,
nor smelt.
Here,
eyes,
familiar with night
no longer have sight.

There is only waiting.
Waiting,
waiting,
waiting.
Is this a vigil?
Then of what feast?
And who or what awaits the waiter?
And who is it that waits?

6

Wisdom's Ways:
The Interior Senses

Our encounter with Wisdom awakens our interior senses at ever deeper levels. These senses are akin to our exterior senses of seeing, feeling. smelling, hearing, tasting, and touching. Each of the interior senses opens us to realizing the presence of divine love from within, an inner experience which may or may not coincide with our external senses or with our emotions. The senses bring us from our formal prayer time into the marketplaces of our lives. Here they help us penetrate life and meet it at its most significant levels. In so doing, they enhance the dailiness of our lives by providing us with sources of enlightenment that carry us beyond the mind sets and perspectives that we perceive with our ego consciousness. These senses also energize and feed our desire and commitment to persevere in prayer and lead us more deeply into the mind and heart of Christ.

We know these spiritual senses through our own experiences and through the lives and histories of our Christian ancestors. Many individuals in the life and tradition of the church have identified these senses as part of divine activity working in them. These senses can be likened to windows of the heart that open within us to various degrees and at different times along the spiritual journey. Once opened, they provide us with a whole other experience of consciousness—a consciousness that touches into divine life itself.

Seeing

Eye has not seen, nor has ear heard,
the great things God has in store,
for those who love God.
—1 Cor. 2:9–10

Francis of Assisi is an example of someone seeing differently. As he traveled along a road in Assisi, he passed a leper sitting on the side of the road. Francis, we are told, then turned, dismounted his horse, went to the leper, and kissed him. In this scenario Francis sees differently; he is not seeing disfigurement and disease, rather he is seeing beneath the skin to the beauty of the person.

"Saints," writes Joan Chittister, "see the same things we see, but they see them differently."

We perceive this gift of spiritual seeing repeated many times in our own day. In our supermarkets we notice parents or other adult companions caring lovingly for persons, either young or elderly, who are dealing with disabling diseases of mind and body. The genuine love and patience these caregivers express highlight the heart's capacity for a different kind of seeing.

Hearing

". . . if you accept my words
and treasure up my
commandments within you,
making your ear attentive to wisdom
. . . then you will find the
knowledge of God."

—Prv. 2: 2

The heart that is moved by hearing a familiar passage of sacred scripture is one whose interior sense of hearing has awakened. This is also true of the people who are able to experience compassion for one who is speaking un-kindly and hurtfully to them. On the exterior level they hear the harsh or violent words that are projected at them, but with their interior sense they hear the other's pain. They know that the pain of self-hatred has many forms and results from not being centered in the experience of one's own whole-ness, goodness, and loveableness, and that the speaker is projecting this inner dis-ease onto them.

We can imagine that Jesus-Sophia knew this kind of experience when he allowed Judas to kiss him immediately before Judas betrayed him. An-other symbol in our own times is the nonviolent and compassionate stance of the Dalai Lama toward the Chinese government and people, even after the government has so murderously and violently occupied Tibet.

Tasting

To him (her) who is without sense she says,
"Come and eat of my bread and
drink the wine I have mixed."
—Prv. 9: 3–5

Tasting is a spiritual sense frequently alluded to on the spiritual journey. "Taste and see," writes the psalmist, "the goodness of the Lord." Directees use this sense to identify spiritual nourishment or its lack. "My soul needs something so I looked for a good spiritual book to appease my hunger." Such a statement is in the direction process. So too, is the expression, "I seem to have lost my taste for spiritual reading," or "I've lost my taste for prayer." Images of food and nourishment find many levels of expression and identify both the inability of the heart to sustain itself on the journey as well as its insatiable desire for spiritual food. "As a deer pants for running water, so my soul yearns for you my God" (Psalm 42).

Smelling

You filled me with your fragrance
and I breathed you in
and breathed you forth.
—St. Augustine, *Confessions*[1]

The spiritual sense of smell is less familiar to most of us now than in ages past when people experienced the odor of sanctity in the presence of our holy foremothers and forefathers. Frequently, however, people today do refer to a period of contemplative prayer as a sweet experience. This means that although they are not conscious of or looking for any experience during this prayer time, they sometimes feel afterwards as if they have been joined to or steeped in an experience akin to a lovely fragrance, to sitting in a garden with the smell of jasmine or heather filling the atmosphere.

Sometimes, too, we speak of certain experiences as having a familiar smell even though there is no odor present. Such cases may refer to an experience in which people sense some divine activity that they have already encountered in the past, such as, "This experience had the smell of a dark night approaching."

---

1. Augustine, *The Confessions*, ed. John E. Rotelle (Villanova, Pa.: Augustinian Press, 1997), 262.

Touching

... Higher still we mounted by inward thought and
wondering discourse on your works,
and we arrived at the summit of our minds;
this too we transcended, *to touch that land of never-*
failing plenty where you pasture Israel forever
with the food of truth.
Life there is the Wisdom through whom all things
are made: and all others that have been or ever will be;
but Wisdom herself is not made:
... in Her there is no "has been" or "will be," but only being ...

—St. Augustine, *Confessions*[2]

Frequently, we read or hear stories that we say are touching. (There is universal agreement about this type of experience. This kind of touching testifies that something deep inside of us was moved or "touched.") When the crowds were pressing upon Jesus-Sophia as he walked through Galilee, he turned and asked, "Who touched me?" For he knew *power* had gone out of him. When we find something "touching," we recognize a change in ourselves. Like a cool breeze on a hot day, a story or event softens, opens, changes the heart.

The more deeply we know companionship with Wisdom, the more will we realize the potential of these interior senses. When the windows of these senses open to us we become awake to Wisdom's presence in us and in our world. Wisdom mothers these senses. She is their wet-nurse and facilitator. Through them she leads us to spiritual knowledge. This knowledge is a knowing that is not dependent on the rational mind, although the rational mind registers and can address this knowing.

The cool breeze
finds a home on even
a single blade of grass
—Issa[3]

2. Ibid., 227.
3. *A Haiku Garden*, ed. Stephen Addiss (New York: Weatherhill, 1996), 45.

The Interior Senses and the Process of Spiritual Direction

The interior senses are important in the spiritual-direction process for both the director and the directee. For the director, every spiritual-direction session is a self-emptying process, one that mirrors the interior disposition he or she brings to contemplative prayer. This disposition involves first, letting go of any personal agenda. When directees sit across from their director, a special time period begins that calls both to an attentive disposition, just as the gong that sounds before a meditation period calls the pray-er to openness and attention. The vibration of this gong locates itself inside the meditator and moves, as it were, in a zigzag fashion to the inner center of the meditator. In each spiritual-direction session, the director centers herself—finds Wisdom's gate, as it were, and then sits in Wisdom's company, attentive and alert to her promptings.

Secondly, the director always, always, sits before the directee in faith and in hope. This means that no matter how much training, education, and skill a director brings to his or her ministry, both director and directee completely depend on Wisdom for any help, insight, or experience of prayer that emerges from the session. Spiritual direction is *always* an experience of ontological poverty for the director, an experience of total dependence on the activity of divine love. A director's insight from a book or article recently read may or may not be helpful to the directee's growth, may or may not be appropriate to the session. There is nothing really to count on or depend on during the session except the inspiration that Wisdom gives as a gift as the session unfolds. *Both* the director and the directee are responsible for discerning where and how Wisdom is moving. The gifts and talents of the director will help facilitate this.

Thirdly, sitting at Wisdom's gate is also an act of hope. There is the director's natural hope that the session be worthwhile, and the supernatural hope one exercises in entering a session without knowing its outcome. Staying in touch with this experience keeps directors very humble and prevents them from claiming any beneficial result in the directee as "their" doing. A good spiritual director knows all is gift.

The spiritual senses are operative in directees as both challenges and consolations.

- Friends may *hear* the voice of love during the session confronting or challenging them with a lack of truth in themselves, or hear, "This is my beloved One," spoken to them as their faith is renewed.
- Friends may *see* again or for the first time their own goodness and divine love's unconditional love for them; they may see their sinfulness, faults, or failings, and discover them to be "happy faults"

because when seen from this interior place they can also be instruments of true repentance. As such, sins or faults can lead directees into the experience of divine love's mercy and compassion, and consequently to the healing of their deep-seated psychic wounds.

- Friends may *smell* the sweetness of the experience of sharing their sacred story with another who genuinely cares for them and knows the content of their story, their behaviors, or their faults does not determine this care.
- Friends may *touch* and be touched by divine life; be changed by the experience because their hearts, once hardened, are now soft and open to life, or because their hearts, once filled with love, now overflow with gratitude and praise also.
- Friends may *taste* and be nourished by the spiritual food that is part of every spiritual-direction session.

It is Wisdom who helps to weave the conversation between friends in spiritual direction. Through her our spiritual senses are awakened, and we begin to know and experience Reality at ever deeper levels.

> Out beyond ideas of wrongdoing and rightdoing,
> there is a field. I'll meet you there.
> When the soul lies down in the grass,
> the world is too full to talk about.
> Ideas, language, even the phrase "each other"
> doesn't make sense.
>
> —Rumi[4]

The interior senses operate in a variety of ways in the director as well. Each spiritual-direction session provides the director the opportunity of seeing inside an individual who is open to the process. The director sees, hears, and touches the pure goodness and lovableness of the friend before her. Each session becomes the holy ground where each knows and experiences divine love's activity in some way. Many directors light candles or incense at the beginning of each session because they want to ritualize this fact. Wisdom's activity in us is a reality intrinsic to life; one keenly experiences her activity in the spiritual-direction process.

In each session the role of the director is to be there for the friend she is with, to be an attentive listener and participant with Wisdom in facilitating her work in the directee. Nevertheless, the director quickly discovers that

4. *The Enlightened Heart: An Anthology of Sacred Poetry*, ed. Stephen Mitchell (New York: HarperPerennial, 1993), 59,

each session mirrors her own story and healing process. The form and content might be very different from her own, but parallels are there. The director needs time for prayer and deep reflection to assimilate what she *sees*, *hears*, and *tastes* within the direction session, time to note how her own heart has been *touched*.

Authentic ministry is always a mutual act of giving and receiving. This is true of each spiritual-direction session in some way, even though the director does not reveal a great deal about herself during the session and does so only when she discerns that this will facilitate the activity of Wisdom in the directee. Projecting too much of her own experience into the session can not only thwart the purpose of the session, but it can also be an experience of the director's ego becoming overly involved and thereby impeding Wisdom's activity. Each session is a self-emptying experience for the director, one in which she lays down her life, that is, her ego and its needs, for the other.

Vapor God

Not empty,
nor full.
Not dry
nor sweet.
Not tomb,
nor womb.
All is vague—
vapid.
I know womb,
its security,
feeding,
nurturing love.
I know tomb,
its stench,
its horror,
your abounding absence.
But this is your cruelest trick,
the meanest yet.
Here,
imprisoned
in your love,
I do not cry out,
scream,
or wrangle to get away.
A dull sadness
dresses my soul.
I neither wait,
nor long for
your presence.

(Too much passion
for a vapor God.)
No, what I do is:
keep on keeping on,
depending on a vapored
knowing.

Neither my voice
nor my hopes raise.
Is this despair?
No demands,
shouts,
pouts,
tantrums,
only unwithheld love—
a love sucked clean
of desire and fulfillment.

Your lessons
coat my everyday.
I miss you deeply,
sorely,
but know your tricks
with water—
like wine and walking.
So,
if vapor is your presence now
I shall love the mists,
the clouds,
the unseen.

7

At Home in Wisdom:

Knowing

Participation in divine life results in the experience of knowing, a foundational religious experience. This is not the knowledge gained through the use of our senses nor the knowledge that involves our rational mind and its ability to think logically, abstractly, and creatively, as when processing information or forming new ideas; nor is it intuition. In the spiritual life we speak of still another form of knowledge. This knowledge is a knowing that is not dependent on the rational mind or on intuition, which is the direct knowledge about *something*. Rather it is an *experience* that results from awakening to Reality, however subtle this experience may be. It is participation *in* divine life which results in the experience of knowing.

This knowing is central to all religious experience and all phases of the spiritual journey. We are reminded here of Jesus-Sophia's own words to the Pharisees after he forgives and cures a person who was paralyzed. "Which is easier to say," Jesus asks the Pharisees, " 'your sins are forgiven you,' or to say, 'Stand up and walk'?" Jesus-Sophia invites his hearers to an experience that goes beyond visible reality. *Knowing* is an experience that does not depend on the rational mind and its powers of logic and reason, or on the emotions, or on any external reality to identify or verify union with divine life. This experience allows individuals to say with a confidence they cannot explain, "I know I am loved; I know God is with me." If people are asked how they know this, they respond, "I just know." This response is a spiritual experience. The person is knowing through the experience of his or her deeper self, no matter how distant or remote this level of reality seems to the conscious mind at the time. Both the director and directee must recognize this experience of union breaking through the layers of human conditioning that block us from the full realization and enjoyment of this truth.

Frequently, when this experience of contemplative consciousness or mystical consciousness is present to an individual through the actions of Wisdom, the experience affects the mind and the emotions. The light that is in the soul breaks through the skin. The joy and happiness that accompany this experience come about because the person is both knowing and feeling their union with holy Wisdom. It is an experience of intimacy and love.

It is very easy for a person to become attached to religious experience for its own sake, that is, for the good feelings it brings with it, and then to try to cling to the experience. If the spiritual director sees this happening during a session, then this becomes a teaching moment in the spiritual-direction process. All or some of the following may then become part of the dialog between these friends.

- All religious experiences are gifts. They are meant to increase faith, invigorate hope, and deepen love.
- To cling to religious experiences for their own sake initiates ego involvement in the experience. This can result not in an increase in faith or love but in narcissism and self-aggrandizement.
- Religious experiences, whether of great import like a vision, or small insight, or a new way of understanding a scripture text, are meant to nurture us in faith as we journey. They sustain us as we mature in faith. A process of liberation accompanies maturity in faith, the liberation of the true self from the dictates and compulsions of the ego. When the ego no longer dominates the spiritual journey or is less involved, people also no longer experience the pleasures and gratification of the ego associated with these happenings. Since for a good part of our lifetimes most of us identify happiness and pleasure with fulfilling the desires of the ego, we may experience the ego's diminished role as a lack, as "something missing." Eventually, however, the experience of knowing will become more meaningful and pleasurable, but not in the same ways the ego once knew. Over time the threads or rope still connecting the ego to spiritual experiences dissolve. The ego and its activity do not dissolve, but our addiction or attachment to the ego gradually lessens.
- A significant learning on the spiritual journey is that we can trust the divine Mother to provide all that we will need for the journey. To keep grasping for experiences means we have not fully surrendered to her love.
  "Therefore I tell you, do not be anxious about your life . . . Look at the birds of the air; . . . your heavenly Father/Mother feeds them. . . . and, indeed God . . . knows you need all these things." Mt. 6:25–34
- Like the laborers in the fields in the gospel parable, some will have more spiritual experiences, others less, and still others, seemingly

none. Wisdom holds all, however, at her breast, suckling all with her pure, life-giving milk. The uniqueness of our relationship with Mother-Sophia, with Christ, with Wisdom, with the divine Father, with the One Who Is will manifest itself in particular and multitudinous ways. The experience of contemplative consciousness is a place of no comparisons or contrast, no hierarchy of experience. Here, the All in All is known; here we experience communion in and with all that is. The person in direction who feels deprived of any religious experience must be helped to find the pure milk of the divine Mother as it is fed to him or her and not want the experience unique to someone else's relationship. To encourage the directee to ask for some nourishment, some way of experiencing that they are indeed loved, is appropriate. Most important, however, is to encourage the directee to detach from preconceived ideas about how these experiences feel. Knowing is a foundational religious experience; feeling the experience is not.

- Since divine love is in the continuous activity of self-giving to us and our world, asking the directee to identify when or where she has realized this in the dailiness of her life is an important part of the direction process. Through it directees become more aware of divine love's activity, and they also become less self-focused.

Our spiritual journey invites us to an experience of love so deep and so profound that it is more than words can ever describe or we can possibly imagine. On this journey Mother/Father God coaxes us through the birth canal of our spiritual life, the canal that leads us from the ego to the true self. This shift in where we locate our identity brings with it both the labor and pain of birth and the freedom and joy of new life. We find this new life in the experience of contemplative consciousness, or communion consciousness, or mystical consciousness. These words express a reality that can't fully be expressed. Here, the self lacks nothing and finds everything. It is the experience of coming home. Every image and experience of a homecoming that is filled with love points to this homecoming, that is, the return of our life's energies to their source, or the discovery of our deeper self. Each contemplative prayer time is our response to love and the pathway to this experience of home. It is Wisdom who leads us home; it is she as divine Mother who welcomes us, and it is she who searches the hills, valleys, city streets, and hospital wards calling our name when we get lost or forget where we live. All religious experiences are gifts; they are Wisdom's guidance and nurturance on the way home. Knowing is the experience of being at home with Wisdom. This knowing will expand and deepen as we mature in faith, as we become one in and with Wisdom. It is this experience of knowing that allows both Paul and ourselves to say: "I live now, not I, but Christ lives in me."

This experience of homecoming allows us to realize our true identity, an identity no longer dependent upon descriptions or modifiers about itself in order to realize its goodness and worth. We no longer need to say, "I am a doctor," or "I am heterosexual (or homosexual)." We discover instead that now our statement of identity reiterates that made by Jesus-Sophia, namely, "I am." It is a statement of our essential nature, our person. It comes from the experience of realized union in and with divine life. It is the experience of simultaneously knowing union and differentiation, oneness and communion, individuality and the interconnection of being. It is the contemplative experience. The experience of contemplative consciousness leads us to the realization that our personal faith journey, while maintaining its personal and unique experience of relationship and faith, is at the same time moving with, and intrinsic to, the global and cosmic pilgrimage of the unfolding universe. As we discover that we are at home in eternal mystery, we also realize that this oneness with Wisdom results in our doing what she does. We become active participants in the unfolding of creation.

Pentecost Dervish

Twirling,
I circle,
hoping
that you
who are fire
will consume
  my fear,
will sear
  my heart,
will brand
  my ego,
will swirl
  me
(like a funnel cloud)
into the still point
  of light,
  of life,
  of love,
  of You.

8

Wisdom's Friendship:
The Dance of Intimacy

The labyrinth, with its maze of concentric circles that eventually leads to the center, expresses the existential experience of persons consciously aware of their spiritual journey. Like so many other journeys that are part of our day-to-day living, this one has times when the traveling seems quite easy and relaxed and times of difficulty and uncertainty. Dawn, morning, midday, evening, night, and dawn again are metaphors identifying experiences of those traveling along this path. The amount of time spent in each phase will vary, as will the degree of consolation or desolation a person experiences. Persons may experience a phase for weeks, months, or years, or experience a certain phase as the overriding experience of their life. These phases are not necessarily consecutive, nor are they onetime events on the journey.

In trying to describe the indescribable, the activity of divine love in relationship to us, these images and descriptions can only hint at and name some of Wisdom's activity in the kitchen of our souls. Our encounter with Wisdom and how she works in and with us will always bear its own uniqueness. In the spiritual-direction process it is helpful for directees to know, however, that what they are going through is part of the spiritual journey and not the result of their imaginations or something they caused. What they are experiencing in their own way has been formally identified as part of divine activity by foremothers and forefathers, such as Teresa of Avila, Julian of Norwich, Thérèse of Liseux, John of the Cross, Ignatius of Loyola, and other great teachers found in the rich tradition of the church.

Dawn

Dawn on the spiritual journey is that moment when an individual awakens to an intuition for the more of life, for some deeper meaning or purpose.

This intuition causes him or her to begin a spiritual search and to make efforts at discovering answers to the questions they find churning inside. Is there a divine Being? If so, how am I related to this Being and how is divine Being related to me? Can I still believe the religion of my childhood and its experience of the Divine? Can I now assimilate this religion with who I am as an adult?

At this stage on the journey the individual moves within toward an interiority which articulates and maintains one of life's ever-present questions: Who am I?

If individuals seek spiritual direction at this stage, it is not so much for help with their prayer life, since that is still nebulous and emerging, but to find help and guidance in their search. An openness on the part of the director to listen to stories and make suggestions about reading materials that will address their search can be helpful. Encouraging the directee to become more familiar with the person of Jesus-Sophia by reflecting on themes and passages of the New Testament is well-suited to this stage. When appropriate, suggesting an eight-day directed retreat may be the path that will provide the directee with the time and space to explore his or her experience of Wisdom's call and the invitation to a personal relationship with Jesus-Sophia. The director can encourage the directees to explore different experiences of prayer that call them to a deeper life and then help them discern the differences between experiences of true prayer and other experiences, such as fads and pseudoreligious practices which entertain or feed their egos.

Morning

Morning is a time of discovery and relief for journeyers. It is a time when they experience a sense of self that is deeper than the ego they have always identified with. It is a time when they enter into their relationship with Jesus-Sophia not as the product of their parental or cultural faith histories but through their own choice. Through prayer and the reading of the gospels and other spiritual books, they explore who Jesus is and begin a personal relationship with him. Like all new relationships, this one brings with it a certain amount of excitement in discovering the other. And as in all new relationships, there is an attraction stage. Here, journeyers see Jesus as an object of their affection, someone to admire, someone to model their lives on, someone perhaps, to receive gifts from.

The journeyers at morning somewhat acknowledge the suppressed or denied fear of death that lurks in the unconscious and which constantly infiltrates our life. Newfound belief that the same Spirit that was in Jesus-

Sophia, leading him through his life, death, and resurrection, is in them and leading them through their own life, death, and resurrection somewhat assuages both the fear of final death and the experience of death that humans face with all kinds of change and growth. This is a hopeful time on a person's journey because she or he begins to sense the possibility of real connection with divine love.

The director at this stage assists Wisdom in her activity of making the reality of Christ's presence more realized. One facet of the direction process at this stage is helping the directees identify from their own lives how and where this same Spirit that is in Jesus-Sophia is leading them.

Midday

One of the most profound stages of the spiritual journey, midday, identifies a place where several great events take place simultaneously. The major event of this phase happens when the person discovers, perhaps during a week's retreat or time of prayer, or while conversing with their spiritual director or another friend, that he or she is in living communication with Christ, not only talking *to* Jesus-Sophia but being addressed in this relationship as well. There is intercommunication, intercourse, relationship with divine love. This is a huge and powerful event in the life of an individual.

The interior senses awaken at this time as well. This awakening enables individuals to experience themselves and the world around them from a different perspective. A shift in where they locate their identity begins. They sense a place of identity free from the cultural, societal, and family patterning that has governed them. They begin to realize a deeper self, their true self, a self that is intrinsically good and whom the divine Other loves unconditionally. The sweetness of the smell of union wafts through them as they sense that their true identity is already in divine love.

Needless to say, this is an ecstatic experience in the life of journeyers. They can believe at this point that they have everything, that there is no place further to go, nothing more to learn. This is a time of consolation in the life of the friend coming for spiritual direction. It is a time for the spiritual director to give the directee the time and space required by these experiences of knowing the palpable gifts of divine love. It is a time for the director not to interfere with the activity of Wisdom but to companion her unobtrusively. A sense of timing is very important here. Frequently, directees tend to level off at this stage and to grasp their newfound experience for its own sake. The director must be aware of this and, when appropriate to do so, remind the directee that all religious experiences are gifts and are not to be clung to as personal possessions. Religious experiences are meant to nourish the soul in faith, in hope, and in love as it moves ever deeper into the full realization of its union in divine love. Clinging to the experiences defeats the purpose for which the gift was given and becomes instead part of the world of the ego and its need for self-aggrandizement and self-preoccupation.

Evening

Most times the evening experience comes upon us gradually. The spiritual tradition of the church knows this time as the "night of the senses."[1] It is a time when one or all of the spiritual senses that directees have delighted in seem to close down or fade away. The strong sense of self they knew at midday now knows the experience of self-doubt and confusion. The encounter with Christ, the felt experience of being in a relationship of mutual love with divine love, seems remote as well. It is a difficult time for directees. They often come to spiritual direction during this time feeling flat, confused, lost. Nothing spiritual engages or fits them. Spiritual nourishment seems to disappear. All seems dry and lost.

The director who recognizes the activity of Wisdom in this dry time will be very helpful to the directee. The director can allay a great deal of fear and concern by identifying what is happening to the directee as part of the spiritual journey. An important role of the director in this case is to name and identify the experience and to provide information about this stage of the spiritual journey through conversation with the directee about this spiritual transition. She reminds the directee that this kind of transition, like the many other transitions experienced in life, means he or she is moving from one spiritual place to another and that this in-between time is always somewhat confusing.

Transitions on the spiritual journey are the pathways to liberation. Since the draw of divine love invites us to ever deeper realizations of intimacy and union, the layers that separate us from our center, a place of realized union, the layers affixed to our egos and its patterning in sin, fear, and guilt, must be peeled away. This process is part of the growth and the deeper experience of love to which the spiritual journey invites us.

The director strongly encourages directees to continue their practice of prayer during this time, "to hang in there" with faith and love. She reminds them that this is a time for faith, a time to trust that it is indeed the draw of divine love they are experiencing and that this call to new life only comes

---

1. St. John of the Cross, *The Ascent of Mount Carmel* and *The Dark Night of the Soul*.

about if we are able to detach from or die to what we have previously known and experienced. Providing directees with an image from sacred scripture to meditate upon that depicts a similar transition, such as Mary Magdalen encountering Christ in the garden and trying to cling to him, or some other reading that addresses this spiritual topic, can help ground directees in the experience of faith necessary during this time.

Night

St. John of the Cross refers to a time beyond the night of the senses that he names the night of the spirit. Nothing of the self seems to remain and all once held as significant seems to dissolve. This night is a time of no experience of any kind except that of death and emptiness. A voluminous sense of absence replaces the once treasured experience of the presence of divine love. All the props which once supported belief—images of the divine Other and the experiences of the spiritual senses—are no longer present. The night of the spirit can be likened to free-falling from an airplane without a parachute. It is an experience that can be horrifying for directees, who often seek spiritual direction at this time. They know the deepest kind of desolation, feeling that they have done something very wrong and have somehow caused the absence of God and the emptiness they are experiencing.

A director's familiarity with and recognition of this experience of night, its darkness and emptiness, is, once again, very helpful to directees. Discovering that this stage is also part of the spiritual journey and that others along the way have experienced something akin to what they are experiencing feels like balm being poured on an open wound for directees.

A good spiritual director will not interfere with the work of Wisdom by trying to take away directees' pain. She will, however, recognize the grieving process that is part of this stage. Since loss of all that one once knew is part of this experience, a certain amount of grieving is appropriate. As in all grieving processes, directees will attempt to get back what has been lost. Frequently, directees will return to geographic spaces where they experienced divine love or to some prayer form or some book or article that once engaged and inspired them in an effort to recapture what now seems lost. Often, they will feel duped or abandoned as their personal relationship with divine love seems to fade and their experience of feeling connected to divine love diminishes completely. The director can help directees express their feelings around what is happening to them and encourage them to write them out or use some form of art, such as drawing, finger paints, or clay, to depict them. It is important to acknowledge the feelings of hurt, betrayal, or abandonment that are part of this stage, but just as important not to wallow in emotions of self-pity for too long a period of time, and thereby identify with the ego at a time when the activity of divine love is trying to draw us beyond our usual ways of knowing and experiencing life. The director recognizes that at this stage, no matter what the emotional response of the directee, divine love is calling the loved one to greater intimacy. Directees can only experience this intimacy if they, like the grain of wheat, die. The directees must not resist the experience but embrace it. The director encourages directees to do this by keeping journals about the feelings they are experiencing and, when they are able, to surrender themselves and these feelings to the divine Mother. She encourages them to live by and in faith; she encourages them to trust that divine love is with them at this time. She explains that they could never know the absence of the divine Other so keenly, if divine life were not already present to them.

Dawn Again

The Christian journey promises us new life whenever we enter into death in faith. This second dawn is a transition from darkness into the light that fills the individual with joy. It is like being lost in a dark tunnel and exiting into light. It is a time of rejoicing. Although everything in the external world seems the same on one level, all is different to persons in this stage because they are different. This difference in them might manifest itself in some or all of the following ways, and to various degrees. Divine light floods their interior senses, a light that reaches deep into the caverns of their hearts and psyches and frees them from the lens of the ego. They begin to realize a new kind of consciousness, an experience in which they realize oneness *in* and *with* divine life and divine consciousness. They identify this experience as mystical consciousness or contemplative consciousness or communion consciousness. It is this consciousness that becomes their center of identity. They find their home, their interior home, in this union with divine love. This experience so deeply marks them, sears them as it were, that their happiness can only be found in being faithful to the love that is reflected in this experience.

The experience of divine Mystery broadens and deepens at this stage. The directees find in the experience of Christ the true meeting of all that is human and divine. They know, not as an intellectual belief but with a different kind of knowing, that divine life is beyond all form. This experience brings them beyond knowing Jesus-Sophia as the object of their affection, as they once did, and also beyond the experience of duality, the subject-to-subject relationship. Contemplative consciousness is an experience of knowing the interiority of Christ's own consciousness, which cannot be observed but only known from the inside. It is an experience of our consciousness uniting with the consciousness of Christ, or the discovery that the *I am* uttered by Christ is the same as our *I am*. The experience of this stage elicits the same response we find in Paul: ". . . it is no longer I who live, but it is Christ who lives in me"(Gal. 2:20).

Persons in this stage return to their daily lives not only with a better sense of Jesus's mission, but *with* that very mission. They know Jesus' mission of healing, redeeming, and liberating now happens through them, that the reign of divine love depends on the community, the body of Christ, bringing it about. Right relationships, doing works of peace and justice, taking actions to bring about systemic change, caring for the earth are no longer moral imperatives. These activities now constitute their identity, an identity experienced as contemplative consciousness.

This stage also brings its human burdens. When divine light floods the interior senses, the paradoxes and contradictions that exist in our world and in ourselves become more visible to us. Spiritual direction at this stage must challenge directees to go beyond the feeling of relief that results from going through the experience of night. Their relief can tempt them to settle for the good feeling they are now experiencing rather than moving into the new life to which divine love calls them. The gift of religious experience can take us beyond what we can will, beyond the rational mind and its powers of knowing, beyond the psyche and its capacities and perceptions, and open to us divine life and activity. Settling in at a place of our own choosing is always an option. We can choose to identify with the world of our egos. The ever-present drive of the ego for self-absorption and self-aggrandizement can easily attach to religious experience and to the spiritual and emotional excitement that often accompany this gift. As a result, we replace the gift of Wisdom to us with our own narcissism.

As is true of all experiences of authentic love and intimacy, so is it true in our dance of intimacy with divine love: divine love will not impose its will on the beloved. We *choose* to be a partner in this dance of love. The gift of religious experience makes explicit or more conscious in us the dance of intimacy to which divine love continuously invites us. We are invited to move beyond our egos and into an ever deeper realization of the experience of union with divine life. It is important, therefore, to *act* on what we know through the gift of religious experience and not merely to become absorbed in the fact that we now know so much more. The insights and revelations of this dawn can tempt the directee to revel in them without acting upon them. The director, unless he or she is truly awake to Wisdom's activity, can get caught in the same temptation. She, too, will feel the relief of dawn's light. She, too, might hesitate to invite the directee to the activity of faith, hope, and love to which the gift invites both of them.

Exploring how the directee's feeling of relief and new insight leads him or her to express gratitude to divine love is one test of faith in action. Noting whether the directee is invited to any specific change resulting from this experience, such as living more simply, more truthfully, or more prayerfully, and then exploring what this might look like concretely, is another. All of this requires a sense of timing on the part of the director and an openness to the discernment process to which both the director and directee are called each time they enter into the spiritual-direction process. Discernment is integral to all of life since all of life involves our choices. The spiritual-direction process formalizes this process and provides us with someone who has the gifts and skills to help us in it.

Dancing: The Ongoing Venture

Divine love continually draws us to new depths, to new experiences of life and love. These entries into divine Mystery are often disorienting to the journeyer, and create an experience of culture shock. Individuals experience culture shock when they have difficulty adjusting to an environment with which they are not familiar. Confronted by the newness and lack of familiarity with the events and circumstances of this new environment, they feel their psyche is being bombarded. Since they don't have categories for these experiences, their minds cannot immediately assimilate what is happening to them. Consequently, they feel lost and disoriented.

Each new stage of the spiritual journey has a disorienting effect on us. The experience of moving ever deeper into the mystery of divine love and our true selves can be a culture shock to body, mind, and spirit. Each phase—dawn, morning, midday, evening, night, and dawn again—will invite us to new depths and an ever deeper expansion of consciousness. The general character of these phases will be the same and become familiar to the journeyer, but the experiences connected to each realization of divine Mystery, her love and her faithfulness, will always be new and call our individual consciousness and our world consciousness into transformation.

Morning 2

Morning 2 in the life of the journeyer is an experience of consolation and depth. A sense of well-being and joy accompanies this experience. Divine light floods the spiritual senses and intensifies awareness of the many paradoxes of our personal lives and life in general. Not only do we experience deeper levels of our true selves but we also experience and see the shadow side of our personalities more clearly. For instance, as we know the experience of being held in Love, we also find ourselves still acting unloving in our words and behaviors. The spiritual director helps directees adjust to experiencing these paradoxes simultaneously. During this stage, our choices seem permeated with visions of the ego and its dynamics and the experience of the deeper self and its call for authenticity. It baffles us when we reflect on the choices we make for the ego, since we now know well that they will not bring us real happiness.

In the morning 2 stage, a time of consolation and new discoveries, the director's main task is to be a listening presence. Directees come to spiritual direction wanting someone to understand and appreciate their experience. If these directees have not already done so, they frequently look now for a more formal contemplative practice of prayer—a practice of prayer that is not confined by words or images. The director can offer to these directees books and tapes that present the Christian path of meditation[2] and, in the following sessions discuss whether or not this way of prayer seems to coincide with the promptings of Wisdom as she addresses them.

Midday 2

An experience of congruence marks the midday 2 phase of the journey. The outside and the inside of the person match. Identifying with their deeper selves enables directees to find their own voices and speak the truth as they know it. They feel at one with who they are and who they are called to be. It is a comforting time for them.

The paradoxes of life observed in morning 2 now become realities inside and outside of them. They are no longer intrigued by the phenomena of these paradoxes because now they are experiencing them simultaneously. They know simultaneously both personal pain and personal joy as the death/ resurrection mystery is revealed in their own life stories. They also know cosmic joy and cosmic pain as the story of our world unfolds. This means they begin to feel in their bodies what is being experienced in the mystical body of Christ. It is a very direct, concrete experience. They cringe at all the violence and cruelty projected on their TV screens and in their own lives. They weep over the sufferings in the Balkans, the Middle East, Africa, on our city streets, in our homes, and in our own relationships. At the same time that they experience cosmic and personal pain, they experience cosmic and personal joy in the wonders and beauty of our universe, in our planet

---

2. Books written by John Main, O.S.B., Laurence Freeman, O.S.B., and Thomas Keating, O.C.S.O., present meditation in the Christian tradition.)

earth, in the joy of nations and friends making peace with one another, in the ever-expanding joy of knowing that they are in the continuous and eternal experience of love.

Their sense of the cosmic Christ encompasses this experience. They are now able to realize in a new way the interconnection of all that is: earth, planets, animate and inanimate matter. They treasure creation in new ways.

"There exists in all beings," says Theilhard, "a common centre" through which "they meet together at a deeper level . . . and we may call this Centre equally well the point upon which converge, or the ambience in which they float [milieu in which they are immersed (Mooney, p. 79)]." This bond of unity constitutes the axis of all individual and collective life. It is in virtue of this axis that we see that Christ has not only a mystical, but a cosmic body. . . . And this Cosmic Body, to be found in all things . . . is eminently the mystical Milieu; whoever can enter into that milieu is conscious of having made their way to the very heart of everything, of having found what is most enduring in it.[3]

Frequently at this phase of the journey, an individual becomes interested in other world religions, finding in them an expansion of the truth of divine Mystery and alternative ways of discussing and relating to divine Mystery. This breadth of knowledge is like a cool breeze on a hot summer's day. It brings comfort and nourishment to believers. It expands their awareness and delight in finding metaphors and images different from their own that nuance and articulate the experience of divine Mystery.

The experience of consolation in midday 2 comes from the directee recognizing that divine Mystery is indeed at work in them and in the world. However, realizing both sides of personal pain and joy as well as cosmic pain and joy, can be disconcerting. The director indicates that this is a time when true humility emerges. As we recognize our choices for egocentricity over and against all that our expanded consciousness now realizes, we sense our own limits. The director helps these friends not to get stuck in self-recrimination for how they perceive themselves *failing* love, and invites them to see their propensity for egocentricity as an impetus for discovering and broadening their experience of divine love. The director points out that this very propensity for egocentricity causes one to seek and find divine mercy and to know a real sense of humility. This experience of realized compassion and mercy broadens and deepens our understanding of divine Mystery and brings us to new levels of self knowledge.

3. Beatrice Bruteau, *Evolution toward Divinity* (Wheaton, Illinois: Theosophical Publishing House, 1974), 56.

Evening 2

In the evening 2 phase of the spiritual journey, individuals lose touch with the rich experiences of what seem to connect us to Wisdom and her many ways. A sense of dread rumbles through individuals as they sense Wisdom is again drawing them into darkness. But this evening experience is not the same as their first one. They now know that the new life they found as the result of the first evening and night experience makes the journey worth any price. Although this is a phase devoid of felt experiences, their "spiritual bank"—a place where faith and the experience of being loved have been preserved and built up over the years, a consciousness filled with a sense of knowing that is not dependent on emotions—confirms them in the belief that they are loved and that Wisdom is indeed with them, guiding them and bringing them to new life in all circumstances.

Because the loved ones know they are loved, they enter this darkness that will once again draw them more deeply into the experience of divine love. Maturity in the spiritual life helps them to know that darkness and light flower in the same garden.

During the spiritual-direction session of the evening 2 stage, the director helps the directees to connect this time of darkness and loss with their first evening and night experience. This dialog helps the directees also remember the new life that resulted from it and, and confirms for the directee that this is a legitimate spiritual experience, one in which they can freely rely on Wisdom's activity of love.

Night 2

Persons in night 2 feel stripped to the bone, left with no defenses, steamrolled spiritually and emotionally. Many on the journey liken this experience of darkness to a descent into hell. Through present events going on in their lives, they see their primitive emotions and behaviors surface from their dark tombs of repression. They feel and know the unaddressed and unhealed parts of themselves. They experience themselves as an open wound. Although the experience seems too much to bear, they surrender to it in faith and love. All that surrounds them seems empty and futile but they trust. They feel desperate and alone. The second night is a time when the power of darkness seems able to extinguish the light. They are like mountain climbers searching frantically for a rock of safety, some place to put their feet and feel secure. However, at the same time, there is also a subtle recognition that the mystery of this darkness reveals presence as well. They begin to accept, then to love the darkness, not for itself, but for the revelations of mystery they begin to realize through it. This is a sign of mature faith, of wisdom.

The director's role in the night 2 stage is one of compassionate witness. He or she knows that the second night can be frightening and disorienting, a time when darkness seems able to extinguish the light. The director encourages the directee to move beyond their fear and to accept the darkness, not for itself, but for the revelation of holy Mystery that is revealed in it. The director reminds the friend before her that trust is the virtue of those mature in the life of faith; that trust means one chooses to believe when all experiences of comfort, delight, and connection with divine love seem to disappear. Trust, she explains, is what the mature in faith do; it is saying yes to what is unknown and cannot be seen. Trust is the gift of a lover to a lover. Nothing more or greater can be extended to the other.

Dawn Again

Exhausted and relieved, journeyers emerge from this hell. Cleansed and purified of some of the blocks of the ego, they are changed. Directees can say only little about this experience because they are no longer observers of themselves; the great split within them is somewhat healed. The armor of their defenses lie before them. They can choose to put them on or not. These defenses are no longer identified with their essence. Their experience of divine love cannot be separated into images, but is reverenced and loved as the eternal Mystery which permeates all that is. This truth motivates them now to do what eternal Mystery does: to love, to give of one's self, to be a cocreator of our world.

Dawn 2 is like an experience of rebirth for directees. It is a transforming experience. The friends seeking spiritual direction at this stage want to be accountable to someone with whom they can share their experience and receive help in living their life in a way that expresses the depth of Love and union they are now experiencing. The spiritual director's role here, and in all spiritual-direction sessions, is to help the individual discern Wisdom's promptings.

Conclusion

In Wisdom's kitchen we learn many things. We discover that dawn, morning, midday, evening, and night will continue to be part of our spiritual journeys as we move ever deeper into eternal Mystery. We realize that we will experience these stages differently at the various phases of our life. We discover that the increase of faith, hope, and love that is part of all authentic religious experience allows us eventually to recognize the draw of divine love in all the events of our life. We learn to love both night and day. In Wisdom's kitchen we know that companionship with her is not dependent on or limited by any experience of our emotions or our intellect. She teaches us how to be a presence of peace and compassion in our world. We discover all these things and so many more while we are in Wisdom's kitchen. But perhaps our most important discovery is we learn to love dancing.

Addendum

A Dialogue with Wisdom

Journal keeping is a wonderful tool for journeying in the spiritual life, for dialoguing with Wisdom at work in our lives. Christian theology teaches us that the same Spirit that was in Jesus-Sophia leading him through his life, death, and resurrection is in us, leading us through our life, death, and resurrection. This experience of Wisdom as guide and presence within each of us is both comforting and helpful. Journal keeping makes us more conscious and available to Wisdom's presence and our own life stories. It is a helpful way of "staying awake" and not getting lost in the overbusiness of each day. It is also a way of helping ourselves when we get stuck or uncentered.

The following journal entry is presented as one way (there are many) of helping ourselves when we feel uncentered. The context that initiated the entry is presented as well as the simple steps in one method identified with this process.[1]

Method

Find some time and a setting where you can be as relaxed and prayerful as possible. Pray that you will be open to the promptings of Wisdom and ask her to guide you during this time.

Write out everything that comes to your mind. Once you begin to write, do so in a stream-of-consciousness fashion; that is without trying to ask the right question or editing the dialog. Remember that the purpose of *this* dialog is *not* to problem solve but to get recentered, refocused. From this

---

1. My thanks to my colleague Sondra Smalley, L.P., who presented this method in her courses on relationships.

centered place we will be in a better position to make decisions and determine what we should or need to do. Usually we must both get recentered
and then stay with this experience for some time before the next step is
clear. The recentering enables us to *see or hear* differently.

Steps

1. We build a bridge with Wisdom by acknowledging her and then
   identifying our concern. ("I need help! I'm in a really bad place.")
2. We allow Wisdom to bridge with us. She identifies with our
   experience compassionately. ("I'm sorry you feel so confused.")
3. We explore through questions. We let the questions of Wisdom
   arise spontaneously. ("Do you want to tell me what is going on?")
4. We fully write our answer to each question raised and allow it to
   emerge unedited. When completed we immediately hear and answer the next question.
5. When all questions have been explored (there is a sense of knowing
   we have completed the exploration) then we allow Wisdom to
   bridge with us again by asking her last question: "Does it help to
   know I am with you in this?"
6. We answer Wisdom's last question yes. Usually, in our exploring
   through questions, we have unearthed some of the repressed hurt,
   fear, doubt, guilt, or whatever else has led us to feeling a lack of
   peace and centeredness. At the end of the dialog our experience of
   ourselves has shifted because of this exploration. Our yes to Wisdom comes from this experience. We feel more at one with ourselves, centered, and more at one with Wisdom.

Circumstance Preceding the Dialogue with Wisdom

It is Friday. Rita and her friend are staying in a beautiful cabin on a lake
until Sunday afternoon. On Monday Rita is to give a presentation to a group
of religious women. She has most of it prepared. She has looked forward to
this time at the lake for months. However, she arrived at the lake cabin
realizing that she still needs two uninterrupted hours of work to finish her
preparation. She knows that unless she does finish this work, the weekend
she has so looked forward to will not be relaxing and her friend Carol will
be disappointed. Rita decides that if she gets up early on Saturday morning
and works on her presentation, her problem will be resolved.

On Saturday morning Rita does get up early and goes into the sitting room to first pray and then begin her work. As Rita begins her prayer she realizes she does not feel well. Her prayer is very distracted and she feels very restless and unsettled. When Carol enters the sitting room Rita feels her friend is infringing upon her time and space. Carol's cheery greeting receives little or no response from Rita. Rita then tries to work on her talk. However, her feeling of malaise prevents her mind from functioning creatively. With this discovery she begins to feels cranky, angry, and upset. After wrestling with these feelings for a while, she then decides to write about her experience by doing a dialog with Wisdom. The following dialog is reprinted from Rita's journal.

R: Well, here I am! I feel awful.

W: I'm sorry you feel so bad.

R: I am trying not to resist my suffering but I'm not doing too well. I tell myself to enter into it, not resist it.

W: What is it that you are suffering?

R: I don't feel good and my mind is not clicking.

W: Is that your suffering? What is underneath it?

R: I have these great ideas. Today was the time I would put them together.

W: Are they your great ideas?

R: Actually, no. No idea "works" by itself. Unless it is "inspiration," it is just globs of words.

W: Are they my truths that enlighten your intellect?

R: Yes.

W: What is your suffering?

R: I'm afraid I shall waste the group's time. They come hungry, expecting to be fed your food. I'm afraid I'll give them empty calories. Food devoid of real nourishment.

W: Is that your real suffering?

R: I think so.

W: What is preventing your thoughts from coming together? Clicking?

R: I don't feel good. My body is not at par, so my mind isn't working well.

W: If there were no talk to give, what would you do with your body?

R: Be with it, nurture it.

W: If you do that, what happens?

R: Then my mind interferes thinking I'm giving in, not responsible, not overcoming myself to do what needs to be done. Then the group suffers.

W: What is it that the group will suffer?

R: Boredom! Asking for bread and getting stones or air (hot).

W: Is it your mind that's interfering with "living into your suffering"?

R: Yes.

W: If you could turn down the volume of your mind, then what?

R: My body would ache but I would be at peace with it.

W: So, is it as though your mind is hollering at your body?

R: Yes.

W: What would happen if you just observed your mind and your body?

R: Could be interesting.

W: Is this mind that you are describing—you?

R: No. It is cantankerous and acting over and against my body. It is a piece of me trying to take control.

W: Is your body—you?

R: No. It is a dwelling place for me.

W: Where are "you" then?

R: Good question.

W: Is the person writing this dialogue—you?

R: Yes.

W: Can you describe this "you"?

R: I am the one seeing all the parts, seeing how they act as an integrated whole or not.

W: When do you lose touch with this "I"?

R: When I identify with or let a "part" take over—like anger or a sick body, or my intellect. It seems to me that my intellect starts accusing, or acting against my emotions or body, and then I begin to resist what is happening to me.

W: Is it always your intellect?

R: Most times. It could also be an emotion that gets in the way, like anger or annoyance. This morning for instance, I was annoyed at Carol because I wanted silence. I wanted to pray. I didn't want to go outside of myself. I didn't want a lot of happy talk; therefore I was real short with her.

W: What was the real issue?

R: My body was sick and my mind didn't want it to be. It wanted everything at "go."

W: So, what were you annoyed at?

R: I couldn't be myself, i.e., "clicking in" to God, myself, or Carol with ease.

W: Where was your resistance?

R: My intellect was hollering at me for not getting to a deep place in prayer, not transcending my feelings.

W: What was going on here?

R: I wanted to be in a deep and prayerful place and couldn't get there. I wanted to feel good and think creatively but I couldn't do it.

W: What was the problem?

R: I cut Carol off, she got hurt and then became quiet. I felt guilty.

W: What was your suffering?

R: I couldn't be where I wanted when I wanted. Then I couldn't be *how* I wanted to be with Carol.

W: Where is the root of the suffering and where is your resistance?

R: I want so much to be at a "deep place," to finish this project brilliantly, and when my will is interfered with, then it triggers responses of intellect and emotions against the interference. Feeling sick was an interference. Carol was an interference.

W: Do you get to the deep place by trying to go there the way you did?

R: Definitely not!

W: Where was the real you in this scenario?

R: The real me is not the one who woke up and, because her body was out of sorts, then let her mind take over with negative thoughts, or thoughts that resisted what was the experience of the body. The real me is not the one put off by not having things the way I want so that prayer happens easily, and then my mind is sharp for work and creativity.

W: Where is your real I?

R: I think it forgot to get up this morning.

W: Where is it now?

R: I am here writing.

W: How is your body?

R: Not great, but I'm all right with it.

W: How are your emotions?

R: Aligned.

W: What about your intellect?

R: Not negative, not hollering. Focused. Just observing.

W: What is the relationship between your intellect and the emotions?

R: My negative emotions seem to get aligned when my intellect stops resisting what is.

W: Okay, then, last round. What does it mean to live into your suffering?

R: To live into my suffering means or could mean—I have to give this more thought—not to become *identified* with the negatively programmed emotions or intellect, but rather to become an observer of body, mind, and spirit, then to detach from assigning meaning, importance, or value to what is observed.

W: What is the point of observing them?

R: Each time we step back from the place of resistance and observe it, we are no longer identified with it, no longer caught in resistance. We acknowledge our experience but through this observation we are now freer to choose how we will be with it.

W: Is this living into your suffering?

R: I think the acceptance of it as something I must deal with appropriately and from a place of freedom is.

W: Does the suffering disappear then?

R: Well, if I have a broken leg that is frequently painful and the cause of great inconvenience, both of these elements will still be true even when I live into my suffering. What changes is me and how I now deal with the pain and with the inconveniences.

W: Is it an attitudinal change then?

R: Yes, I would say so. And once that changes in me, my feelings about the experience change also.

W: How are you doing right now?

R: Much better.

W: What are you feeling about the situation now?

R: I feel as though I can accept it a little better. The fact is I don't feel good and I can't do the rest of the presentation the way I would like.

W: Does it help to know I am with you?

R: Yes, thank you. I appreciate this gift. It has really helped me. I am very grateful.

When Rita closes her journal she is in a different frame of mind. She is more at one with herself, her body, her intellect, her spirit, and her friend Carol. The way to purifying our minds and hearts is through a process of detachment—detachment from the illusions, delusions, and the negative programming imbedded in us since infancy that continues into our adult life. Detachment is a key virtue to be practiced as part of our spiritual journeys. Detachment means we die to or let go of identifying with our egos and their dynamics and allow Wisdom's loving gifts and presence to draw us into union. Here, our body, mind, and spirit know truth and we find our true home, our true identity; here we identify not with our ego and its programming, but with the deeper self, the true self. This shift in where we locate our identity happens over time and through the activity of Wisdom and our conscious participation with her in this activity. The process of spiritual direction is one way of making this process conscious, journal writing is another.

Rita's dialog with Wisdom identifies a process of detaching from the ego. In the Christian tradition this practice of detachment is seen as our participation in the ongoing death/resurrection mystery of Christ. Sacred scripture identifies this for us in these texts:

> Unless a wheat grain falls into the ground and dies,
> it remains only a single grain;
> but if it dies,
> it yields a rich harvest.
>
> —Jn. 12:24–26

If we have died with Christ, then we shall live with Christ.
. . . If we are faithless, Christ is faithful still.

—2 Tm. 2:10–13

Anyone who wants to save their life will lose it;
but anyone who loses their life for my sake will save it.

—Lk. 9: 23–26

This same process of detachment is highlighted in other world religions as well. For example, in the *Dhammapada*, the Buddha has this instruction:

> We are what we think.
> All that we are arises from our thoughts.
> With our thoughts we make the world.
> Speak or act with an impure mind
> And trouble will follow you
> As the wheel follows the ox that draws the cart. . . .
> Speak or act with a pure mind
> And happiness will follow you
> As your shadow, unshakable.

The dying referred to in these sacred scriptures and so many other texts is the ongoing process of detaching from the ego; a process intrinsic to every seeker who hears Wisdom's call to plumb the depths they are called to and to experience themselves in a reality not dictated or obscured by egocentricity. Wisdom's invitation to come in leads those who follow her to joy, to peace, to true happiness, to oneness with their own being, to the experience of interconnection of being with every person and with all that is. Through this union we begin to realize and experience divine union and to know that we are held in divine love now and always.

Hymn to the Great Mother
(Pentecost Prayer)

Humanity is poised—
  standing on tip-toe
peering over the fence of life
vigilant—
wanting to see, to know
if now is the time,
if here
  is where
You will appear.

Breath is baited,
  stomachs tight,
eyes are focused,
ears alert.
Senses strain,
pain
with anticipation,
with cautious delight.

All is ready.
Desire is ripe.
Hearts are thrown open
yearning,
burning,
for your kiss.

Come,
  come.
Breakthrough.
Pour-out Yourself.
Sophia us.
Mantle us in love.
Bend over,
bend into our vacant spirits.
Subsume us.

O Holy Mother,
be Mother to us.
Feed us,

suckle us with
your milk.
Envelop us,
cuddle us.
Tell us a better story.
This one is too hard,
too long,
too painful,
too much to bear.

Great Mother,
open our senses
to your touch.
Womb us.
Give eyes
  your sight.
Breathe us.
Give ears
  your hearing.
Lead us.
Give touch
    your compassion.
Kiss us.
Slake our thirst,
  bathe us.
Douse your fragrance,
your blessings
upon us.
Soak us through and through.

Holy Mother,
Jesus Sophia,
Mother us—
  (Mother me).
Come,
come,
all is ready,
we are ready.
Don't fail us

in hints and promises.
Splash into
the ocean of our longing.
Wet nurse us.
Our feeding time is past.
Long past!
Hear our cries.

Lean over us.
Draw us into You.
One us in Your love.
Holy Mother,
Mother us.
　Mother me.
Come.

The World Community for Christian Meditation

Meditation creates community. Since the first Christian Meditation Centre was started by John Main in 1975, a steadily growing community of Christian meditators has spread around the world.

The International Centre in London co-ordinates this world-wide community of meditators. A quarterly newsletter, giving spiritual teaching and reflection, is sent out from London and distributed from a number of national centers, together with local and international news of retreats and other events being held in the world-wide community. An annual John Main Seminar is held.

The International Centre is funded entirely by donations and especially through a Friends of the International Centre programme.

The World Community for Christian Meditation / International Centre /
23 Kensington Square / London W8 5HN / United Kingdom
Tel: +44 171 937 4679   Fax: +44 171 937 6790
E-mail: wccm@compuserve.com

Web Page

Visit The World Community for Christian Meditation Web site for information, weekly meditation group readings, and discussion at: **www.wccm.org**

Christian Meditation Centre / 1080 West Irving Park Rd / Roselle IL 60172.
Tel/Fax: +1 630 351 2613

John Main Institute / 7315 Brookville Rd. / Chevy Chase / MD 20815.
Tel: +1 301 652 8635   E-Mail: wmcoerp@erols.com

Christian Meditation Centre / 1619 Wight St. / Wall / NJ 07719.
Tel: +1 732 681 6238   Fax: +1 732 280 5999
E-mail: gjryan@aol.com

Christian Meditation Centre / 193 Wilton Road West / Ridgefield / CT 06877.
Tel: +1 203 438 2440   E-mail: Internet:pgulick@mci2OOO.com

The Cornerstone Centre / 1215 East Missouri Ave. / Suite A 100 / Phoenix / AZ 85014-2914.   Tel: +1 602 279 3454   Fax: +1 602 957 3467
E-mail: ecrmjr@woddnet.attnet

Medio Media Ltd.

Medio Media Ltd. is the publishing arm of the World Community for Christian Meditation.

A catalogue of Medio Media's publications—books, audio sets, and videos—is available from:

Medio Media / 15930 N. Oracle Road # 196 / Tucson / AZ 85739.
Tel: +1 800 324 8305   Fax: +1 520 818 2539
Web page: www.mediomedia.com